RETHINKING WRITING INSTRUCTION
IN THE AGE OF AI

RETHINKING WRITING INSTRUCTION IN THE AGE OF AI

Randy Laist

with contributions from
Nicole Brewer, Cynthia J. Murphy,
and Dana Sheehan

© 2024 CAST, Inc.

All rights reserved. No part of this publication may be reproduced, stored in a retrieval system, or transmitted in any form or by any means, electronic, mechanical, photocopying, recording, or otherwise, without the prior permission of the Publisher.

ISBN (paperback): 978-1-943085-10-1
ISBN (ebook): 978-1-943085-11-8

Library of Congress Control Number: 2023948218

Interior and Cover Design: Happenstance Type-O-Rama

Published by CAST Professional Publishing,
an imprint of CAST, Inc.,
Lynnfield, Massachusetts
USA

For information about special discounts for bulk purchases, please email *publishing@cast.org* or visit *publishing.cast.org*.

This book is dedicated to all of the writing teachers out there. Thank you for your deep sense of purpose, your passionate empathy for students in all their variability, and your commitment to nurturing the values that make and keep us human.

Contents

Introduction 1

Part I: Theory: Universal Design for Writing 11
    Engagement 17
        Access to Engagement. 19
        Building Engagement 21
        Internalizing Engagement. 22
    Representation. 24
        Content-Oriented Instruction 26
        Texts: Readings, Research Sources, and Models of
            Composition. 27
        Feedback to Student Writers. 30
    Action and Expression 32
        Physical Action 34
        Expression and Communication 36
        Executive Function 38

Part II: Practice: UDL-Informed Writing Activities 41

    Building Community 43
        Icebreaker Profile 45
        DIY Writing Handbook 52
        Writer's Vision Board 61
        Writing Journal Blog 70

    Inspiration and Brainstorming 79
        Me-Time Log 81
        Random Fact Fantasia 88
        Multidisciplinary Wonderball 95

    Research. 105
        Show-and-Tell Multimedia Bibliography 107
        Email an Expert 119

Outlining **125**
    My Human Thesis 127
    Outsourcing Your Outline 134
    Index Card Shuffle. 140

Drafting **149**
    Collaborative Paragraph Drafting 151
    Scripting an Instructional Video 157
    Research Roundup Podcast. 164
    AI-Informed Drafting 170

Revision **179**
    Steered Peer Review 181
    "Wraparound" Feedback and Guided Revision 188
    Publish and Flourish. 194
    Talk Show: Featured Writers Segment 201

Acknowledgments **209**

Appendix: UDL Guidelines **211**

Index **213**

About the Author **223**

About the Contributors **225**

Introduction

Writing is an invaluable academic skill, but it is also much more than that. It is a tool for thinking, a means of personal expression, and a vehicle of self-discovery. People engaged in the act of writing put words to vaguely felt intuitions, they contribute to the store of human knowledge and possibility, and they plumb the depths of their own consciousness. Despite the intellectual, interpersonal, and psychological value of writing, however, too many students, and too many people in general, feel shut out of writing. They say things like "I'm just not a writer" or "I'm more of a math person." Their minds go blank in front of a keyboard. They have cold sweats and self-doubt. Sometimes they have the impression that there is some secret that they never learned, or some gate that they were never given the key to. They feel paralyzed by a fear of exposure, embarrassment, and ridicule. They are tempted to have a chatbot ghostwrite on their behalf or to resort to some more traditional form of plagiarism. Maybe you know someone who feels this way, or maybe you yourself cope with borderline graphophobia. The prevalence of this dread of writing poses a challenge to educators to teach writing in a way that makes it seem less like a burdensome threat and more like a natural way of working with ideas.

With its emphasis on identifying and eradicating barriers to learning, Universal Design for Learning (UDL) provides a framework that can help empower student writers. In many ways, UDL is particularly well suited to the teaching of writing. UDL and composition instruction both emphasize the voice and subject-position of individual students, and the "process" model of writing instruction that is common in composition classrooms provides the kind of scaffolded learning experiences espoused by UDL-based pedagogy. At the same time, however, there is also a tension between the composition classroom's focus on the medium of textual writing and the priority that UDL places on allowing students to explore multiple means of self-expression. In a writing classroom, the means of expression *is* the course content, putting UDL-informed writing teachers in the awkward position of balancing the availability of video, audio, and graphic forms of expression against what may sometimes seem like an antiquated commitment to teaching students to write sentences and paragraphs.

One way out of this dilemma is to define writing in a way that encompasses composition in other media. To be sure, new media of communication have expanded the definition of what it means to write to include the design of video, audio, and graphic representations of ideas. Productions in any of these formats require many of the same skills as writing an academic paper, such as identifying a message, establishing a consistent tone, and organizing information within a rhetorical framework. This multimedia approach to composition enables students to cultivate an appreciation for the ways that different forms of communication can shape the presentation of a message, and it also allows students to experiment with forms of communication that reflect their own educational goals and personal styles of self-expression.

At the same time, UDL principles can also facilitate instruction in text-based composition—that is, writing in the traditional sense. The writing process as typically taught involves several stages—prewriting, researching, organizing, drafting, revising—each of which presents students with various challenges. One of the great values of the process approach is its continual reminder that effective writing is always the result of patient sustained effort, demystifying the idea that some students (and some teachers) have about writing that it is the result of some inherent gift or natural talent. There is nothing natural about writing. Indeed, it may be one of the most unnatural things that people do, and it is not surprising that it can be so challenging to do at all, let alone to do well. The process approach recognizes the groping, emergent, always-unfinished quality of writing as an active, ongoing process of discovery. Thinking about the stages of the writing process through a UDL lens can help writing instructors design activities that make each stage more accessible to more students. Even as the final goal of a writing project might be a written text, alternative forms of composition can enhance the substages of the writing process in ways that provide multiple means for students to engage with the material and express their ideas.

"AI-Proof" Writing Activities

The world of composition instruction is abroil with chatbot panic. Now that widely available AI programs can write a five-paragraph research paper on any topic in seconds, writing teachers around the world discover that the ground is shifting beneath their feet. How can they convince students that the grueling labor of writing is worthwhile when the internet can do it for them—indeed, can produce writing of a technically far superior quality to anything they could do themselves, even with weeks of strenuous effort? The faction of "prohibitionists" attempting to find ways to deny students access to these technologies, either by requiring them to write in person or by using AI-scanning plagiarism software (or by any other means), are clearly fighting a rearguard action in an unwinnable campaign. This technology is here to stay, and is sure to become more accessible, more powerful, and more adaptable over the years and decades to come. The questions asked by compositionists should not be how to bypass the impact of chatbot tech, but how to embrace it as an opportunity for us to rethink what writing is for, why it's worth teaching and learning, and even, on a basic level, what writing is.

Fortunately, UDL provides an educational philosophy centered on adaptability to change. In their acute focus on the student experience, UDL-informed educators are continually reassessing their practice in light of how different students respond to the curriculum, how different learning environments pose unique constellations of challenges and opportunities, and, of course, how changing technology impact teaching and learning. The original acronym of the pioneering UDL organization, CAST—the Center for Applied Special Technologies—reminds us that adapting technological innovations to educational situations was one of the historical impetuses behind the development of UDL, and this perspective encourages us to think about how chatbots and other AI-enhanced programs can promote educational possibilities.

When pocket calculators became widespread in the 1980s, math teachers were faced with a similar existential crisis. If the machine can perform calculations instantaneously and flawlessly, what was there left for math teachers to teach? Of course, innovative math teachers recognized this technological development as an opportunity to liberate math from the drudgery of rote calculation, opening up instructional opportunities to explore the much more compelling intricacies at the heart of mathematical inquiry.

It is easy to discern the parallels to the impact that chatbots are having in the composition field. There is a rote quality to routine composition assignments that recalls the impersonal busywork of multiplication worksheets. Arguments, genres, rhetorical formulas, and stylistic choices come prefabricated, or at least predetermined, and the successful student is the one who can paint by the numbers effectively enough to produce a piece of writing that most closely resembles "the right answer" for a particular writing task. Indeed, this is exactly what chatbots do so successfully: mimic the formula that has been reiterated millions of times by previous writers. To be fair, in the same way that facility with multiplication problems was indeed a worthwhile skill in the precalculator days, this kind of writing was also important to the skillset of a prechatbot writer. But now that the chatbots can do our rote writing assignments for us ("Write a five-paragraph essay in favor of gun control," or "Describe the stages of cell division," or "Analyze the color symbolism in *The Great Gatsby*"), writing students and teachers are free to expand into the "higher mathematics" of writing, to do the creative work of reimagining writing instruction—and maybe even writing itself—in ways that make it more meaningful, more authentic, and more human.

The goal of the "AI-proof" assignments in this book is not specifically to prevent students from "cheating," but to structure composition activities that engage students on personal and interpersonal levels. The idea is not to make it impossible to cheat, but to make writing activities maximally meaningful and worthwhile so that students aren't inclined to cheat. As soon as it occurs to a student (or a professional writer, for that matter) that what they are writing could just as easily be written by a machine, it is only rational for them to consider this option. But when writers use writing as a way of examining their own lives and thoughts, when they use writing to communicate with one another about things that matter to them, when they use writing as a platform for their own voices and their own personalities, the fact that chatbots exist becomes as irrelevant to the writing situation as the existence of pocket calculators. At the same time, this moment provides an opportunity for academic writing itself to rediscover the relevance and freshness that have always been the soul of meaningful composition instruction.

The activities in this book implement three strategies for taking advantage of the post-chatbot landscape:

★ The assignments embrace **multimodality**. As discussed previously in this introduction, this book focuses on textual writing as a privileged outcome, but it contextualizes this outcome among the many other kinds of expressive fluencies that constitute contemporary literacy. Activities encourage students to incorporate interpersonal and group conversations, oral presentations, audiovisual technologies, photography and infographics, digital tools, and even chatbots into their writing process in ways that enrich and diversify their engagement with writing projects. At the same time that this multimodal emphasis reflects the working experience of real-world writers, it also makes it impossible for students to rely on a chatbot to do their thinking for them.

★ The assignments are **process-oriented**. The predominance of the process approach in composition pedagogy has fostered classroom environments that nurture developing writers, that encourage risk and growth, and that cultivate metacognitive reflection. It has also always acted as a tool for preventing plagiarism, and, practiced thoughtfully, it can also eliminate the ability of students to pass off chatbot text as their own writing. When instructors get to know a student writer's personal writing style, and when the student writer's work passes through successive stages of development, the utility of chatbots for cheating purposes diminishes considerably.

★ The assignments are **personalized**. This is the most important element to the "AI-proofing" of writing assignments, and it also has the most profound implications for the future of writing instruction. The quality that makes human writing more worthwhile than chatbot writing is the fact that it expresses the emergent, ambiguous, and embodied perceptions of a person with a unique background, a unique way of being in the world, and a unique relationship with whatever they happen to be writing about. The prevailing style of so-called academic writing has traditionally dissuaded student writers from examining the uniqueness of their perspective, preferring the third person to the first, the standard jargon to the eccentric idiom, and the "brain floating in space" perspective to the perspective of lived experience. As computers do more of our writing for us, it is an opportune moment to reimagine academic writing in ways that allow it to become a more vibrant vehicle for human meaning. Again, the purpose is not merely to prevent students from cheating (although asking students to write from their human perspective is a very effective way to obviate chatbot plagiarism) but to seize the opportunity to empower students to use writing to understand themselves, their world, and the connections that hold them together.

The strategies that prevent chatbot abuse are the same strategies that have always characterized effective composition instruction. Instructors and instructional designers who are working to revise their practice in response to the emergence of chatbots can welcome the process as an opportunity to reinforce their commitment to ideals that are central to both composition theory and UDL: relevance, engagement, accessibility, and the empowerment of human potential.

How to Use This Book

This book arose out of a very specific cluster of circumstances. The school where I have taught English for most of my career, Goodwin University, has always distinguished itself by its focus on applying innovative solutions to educational challenges. Over decades, the university has developed an institutional culture that embraces nontraditional students, first-generation students, students whose first language is not English, adult learners, veterans, students with disabilities, and other kinds of learners, and this commitment made Goodwin one of the early adopters of UDL-informed practice. Over many years of teaching writing classes at Goodwin, I've developed a capacious bag of tricks that I use to communicate to students from all backgrounds that their voices matter and to empower them to use their voices to generate new ideas, express their truths, and communicate with one another and with the world beyond. Goodwin's adoption of UDL as an institutional pedagogy freed the curriculum from many "heritage" practices that have been common in higher education for generations prior, challenging the faculty to design classroom experiences that are responsive to the dynamic needs of an ever-changing student population.

More recently, I became the chair of the English department at the University of Bridgeport, a more traditional university that had recently committed to the goal of incorporating UDL-informed pedagogy into its institutional culture. I found myself looking back through my bag of tricks, trying to think of ways to communicate some of what I'd learned about UDL-informed composition instruction to writing instructors who had never heard of UDL before. At the same time the dramatic appearance of AI chatbots on the scene created a new demand for reconsidering traditional approaches to academic writing. In 2020, when the Covid-19 pandemic emptied college classrooms, Goodwin's foothold in UDL practice gave it an advantage over other schools, because we had already been incorporating multiple means of instruction (crucially, online course shells) across all our classes, so the switch over to an entirely online format was not as disruptive as it might have been. UDL gave us the flexibility to adapt to change and survive.

As chatbot panic upends the traditional writing classroom, I once again have the feeling that the UDL approach mitigates the disruptive force of change, since the kinds of writing assignments that are rendered irrelevant by chatbot technology are the same kinds of "one-size-fits-all" assignments that UDL has always sought to transcend. As I talked with writing instructors at the University of Bridgeport about how to address the challenge to traditional practice represented by chatbots, as I developed new content for undergraduate writing classes, and as I have continued to work with a "post-AI" generation of new students, I began compiling this handbook of go-to writing activities—all of which I have overseen in college classrooms at one time or another—in the interest of being able to share them with other faculty. I have already been using this handbook extensively in a number of ways, not only by teaching activities straight out of the book in my own classrooms, but also by building them into Canvas shells and sharing them with other instructors as models of the kind of teaching I hope they do in their own classrooms. With the publication of this book, I hope that these activities can continue to spark ideas and inspire new creative solutions for other writing instructors at other educational institutions, levels, and contexts.

The activities in this book are all loosely structured in ways that make them adaptable to different writing students in different educational contexts. In all cases, the activities are content-neutral—they provide things that students can do with ideas, rather than giving them ideas to do things with. The activity instructions all assume that students are bringing their own thoughts, their own research, and their own questions to these assignments, although if there is specific input or content that an instructor wants students to write about—in a theme-based composition class, for example, or a Writing Across the Curriculum (WAC) context—the activities can be set up so that they help students find their own ways of thinking and writing about the target topics. The activities are arranged according to the stages of the writing process, and they can be combined in different ways so that students may use one activity to structure their brainstorming process, another for outlining, and still another for revision, but they can also be used more sporadically according to the instructor's priorities or the students' needs. For instructors experimenting with a UDL +1 approach—applying one additional UDL component to your teaching—any of these activities can be implemented alongside other instructional techniques. At the same time, these activities can serve as the structure for an entire curriculum in process-oriented composition techniques.

This book is intended to stimulate ideas not only for students but also for instructors, offering a variety of creative strategies for centering student perspectives and scaffolding the development of writing skills. Although the directions aim to be as explicit as possible, different instructors should feel empowered to adapt these activities in whatever ways make sense to them. Steps can be cut out or simplified, instructions can be modified to reflect desired instructional outcomes, and activities can be combined, revised, or exploded; this book is more like a playset than a toolkit or a cookbook. Part I, on theory, articulates ideas for using UDL principles to generate more ideas about how to make composition more engaging and more accessible for more students. Writing classes provide a powerful opportunity to listen to students' voices and to achieve a glimpse into their inner worlds. Responsive and inclusive writing instruction requires us to invite students to use their voices, and it obliges us to listen carefully to what they say, to believe in them, and to learn from them. The ultimate goal of all writing instruction is to stimulate the joy of self-expression in both students and teachers, and to celebrate the universal variety of human voices and the unlimited potential of the human imagination.

Part I

Theory: Universal Design for Writing

Mapping the stages of the writing process onto the UDL Guidelines opens up an enormous wealth of suggestions for how to provide options to support students as they encounter various challenges and attempt to develop their thoughts and feelings into sentences and paragraphs.

The chart on the next page lists strategies for thinking about the various stages of the writing process through a UDL lens. Different instructors who teach writing to different kinds of students in different educational contexts will likely have different questions they would articulate in the cells of this chart, and they would likely identify different instructional strategies in response. The watchword of all UDL-informed practice is *variability,* and this variability encompasses not only the diversity of students but also that of teachers, educational environments, and cultural contexts. One of the most productive elements of UDL is its emphasis on variety, individuation, expansiveness, and multiplicity, and the application of UDL to any particular classroom setting is always an opportunity to experiment with new ideas, to explore creative possibilities, and to pioneer original approaches.

The same can be said of writing instruction, and even of writing itself, which is always a matter of stepping out into the unknown. In the context of the writing class, designing for variability means acknowledging and celebrating the fact that every writer is different, every writing task is different, and every writing context is different. A writing classroom that encourages students to play with different ways of interacting with information and different styles of expressing their own ideas reflects the ever-evolving variety of contemporary communications media as well as the diversity inherent among student writers themselves. In practice, this means designing opportunities for students to play with their ideas and their writing in multiple contexts and formats, individually and collaboratively, verbally and visually, textually and orally, spontaneously and reflectively, independently, and in conversation with peers, experts, online communities, and even chatbots.

For this reason, Universal Design for Writing (UDW) is characterized not by some specific curriculum or activity sequence but by a basic commitment to the variability inherent among student writers. Designing for this variability requires open-mindedness, flexibility, and a basic faith in the belief that every student has a universe of possibilities latent within them.

STAGE OF THE WRITING PROCESS	ENGAGEMENT	REPRESENTATION	ACTION AND EXPRESSION
Brainstorming	Key question: How do students develop a meaningful personal connection with their writing?	Key question: How does the learning environment provide models of brainstorming techniques?	Key question: What media are available for students to convey the results of their brainstorming process?
	UDL strategy: Encourage students to develop writing projects around topics that are personally meaningful.	UDL strategy: Work with students to brainstorm techniques for brainstorming, then practice using these brainstorming techniques.	UDL strategy: Provide students with a menu of options for sharing their insights and ideas.
Research	Key question: What kinds of sources of information will be most likely to engage students' interest about a topic?	Key question: How can multimedia research sources help make information about a topic more accessible to more students?	Key question: How do students record, compile, and assess information from their research sources?
	UDL strategy: Empower students to start with what they know. Where do they find information about topics that are important to them?	UDL strategy: Urge students to draw information from diverse media and to consider their comparative advantages.	UDL strategy: Assign a multimedia portfolio of research sources and create opportunities for students to discuss their research process with their peers.

STAGE OF THE WRITING PROCESS	ENGAGEMENT	REPRESENTATION	ACTION AND EXPRESSION
Drafting	Key question: What incentive do students have to write? Who are they writing for, and why?	Key question: How do students receive information about addressing sentence- and paragraph-level writing challenges?	Key question: How can a student's written text be complemented by or scaffolded around multimedia texts?
	UDL strategy: Encourage students to reflect on their sense of purpose. Why is the topic important to them? Why should it matter to other people?	UDL strategy: Provide opportunities for students to draft paragraphs in a classroom setting where the instructor and their peers are available to suggest solutions for working through challenges.	UDL strategy: Encourage students to outline a piece of writing around images, graphs, or notes for an oral presentation.
Revising	Key question: What incentive do students have to express themselves with precision and professionalism?	Key question: How is feedback communicated to student writers?	Key question: How can the revision process incorporate strategies for publishing key ideas in multiple media?
	UDL strategy: Provide publication opportunities for student writers within and beyond the classroom environment.	UDL strategy: Use multiple media for providing both sentence-level and holistic feedback to student writers.	UDL strategy: Encourage students to develop their writing projects into other media to reach a broader audience.

UDW assumes that:

★ every human being necessarily has their own perspective to share, their own stories to tell, and their own voice to claim; and

★ the writing classroom, as well as global human civilization, becomes richer and more truthful as more individuals contribute their own points of view to a collective conversation.

A writing class is a uniquely meta-educational environment. Rather than just being another subject alongside history and calculus, where the students learn things that have already been figured out by other people, writing classes emphasize the learners' own agency as thinkers and discoverers. History and calculus teachers will maintain that they also teach metacognitive skills through the language of their own disciplines, but in a writing class, the metacognitive element is virtually the entire curriculum. The students themselves are the curriculum of any writing class—their own attitudes and assumptions, their own ways of thinking and of working, their own feelings about themselves and their worlds. While a writing class may involve other instructional objectives, the ultimate goal is always to help students identify their own point of view on a subject and put words to their own impressions and intuitions.

Thinking about writing instruction through a UDL lens suggests a variety of strategies for encouraging students to discover what they want to say and for supporting them as they work to find ways of saying these things that are true to their own experiences. As they work through their writing processes, students ask themselves what they think; find a language to express what they think; communicate with other people about what they think and how they have expressed it; identify more comprehensive, precise, and persuasive language to refine and expand the way they express what they think; and even reassess what they think and why they think it, becoming more reflective and thoughtful versions of themselves. As they perform this difficult work, they inevitably accomplish other goals that are often associated with writing classes: engaging in critical thinking, locating sources of information, reading and interpreting what other people have written, communicating effectively with other people, and practicing the conventions of rhetoric and persuasion. A framework for a UDW embraces all these goals, while also stressing the accessibility of the written word as an expressive possibility for all students. Students who feel empowered to write discover a bottomless source of inspiration, intellectual autonomy, and self-understanding. Applying the principles of Universal Design to the writing classroom can help more students find their voices as writers.

It is also worth noting that, as transformative as a UDL-informed pedagogy can be for writing students, it also provides dynamic possibilities for people who teach writing classes at any level. "Legacy" practices in the composition classroom typically require the writing instructor to provide line edits and personalized commentary in response to stacks of student papers, which all come due at the same time, are frequently about the same topic, and strive to imitate an impersonal rhetorical persona. It is easy to understand how instructors can get burned out under this kind of Sisyphean routine, and also how they might come to question the value of composition classes altogether, especially in an age when any cheap phone can instantaneously produce a persuasive essay about gun control or a research paper about sexism in advertising that would garner straight A's in their classrooms (and the phone would also likely be better behaved, more reliable, less mouthy, etc.). When writing teachers take on a UDL-informed mindset, with its emphasis on innovation, student variability, and multiple means of expression, the factory model of writing instruction is replaced by a model of a writing classroom that is a vibrant crucible of human energies, possibly one of the most stimulating, challenging, and inspirational settings that human beings are capable of participating in. In the UDL-informed writing class, students and teachers work together at the common task of analyzing their shared experience, thinking empathetically about one another's worldviews, testing the limits of language and self-expression, and boring down to find out who we really are, where we're really going, and how we invent ourselves and our societies out of these eternal questions.

While implementing some of the UDL-inspired activities in this book, or making up your own, may involve a certain commitment of planning and time, activating a UDL mindset rewards this investment handsomely. Not only do student-centered composition strategies frequently involve correcting and grading routines that are less repetitive and time-consuming, but they also become animated with the diverse voices of student writers addressing relevant issues in impactful ways. Writing students and writing instructors share the same gross neuroanatomy, after all, and writing instructors often struggle with the same challenges in their own writing that students face in theirs. The same strategies, therefore, that engage a wide variety of students are also likely to engage a wide variety of instructors, and the same strategies that empower students to find and use their own unique voices empower writing instructors in the same way. It is my hope that the activities and perspectives included in this book will not only embolden students to express themselves as authentically as possible, but also inspire writing instructors to explore ways of teaching that they find meaningful and motivational.

Engagement

Engagement is the first and most important step in any educational experience and, really, in any human endeavor. If you are excited about what you are doing—for whatever reason—that excitement gives you the motivation to push through obstacles, it gets your brain working, and it creates the conditions that make success possible. Conversely, when a project seems overwhelming, irrelevant, or tedious, obstacles appear insurmountable, the brain rebels and shuts down, and the possibility of success shrivels conspicuously. While this dynamic is true across all of human life, it is uniquely germane to the task of writing. When writers write with confidence and creativity, it is because their personalities, worldviews, and personal goals become aligned with what they are writing. Meaningful writing, thoughtful writing—the kind of writing that writing teachers want their students to do—can be achieved only by students who are able to find the personal connection that allows them to invest themselves in what they are saying and to make the writing project a kind of extension of their own personal identity. In this frame of mind, writers put themselves into their writing; they transcend formulaic ways of thinking and take creative chances; they care about the words, sentences, and ideas they express; and their writing is charged with purpose and feeling.

My personal feeling as a writing teacher is that achieving this state of emotional involvement in their writing should be the foremost goal for writing students. If they can develop this kind of relationship with their writing, even if intermittently, then the rest of what they need to know about writing will take care of itself. If they care about what they're writing about, they will eventually develop a subsidiary interest in whether the commas are in the right place and other technical questions. Engagement is the magic key that unlocks the rest of what there is to know about writing. But, even more importantly, this feeling of being engaged in one's writing is the elemental experience not only of what writing is and what it is for, but also of what thinking is and what intellectual work is, and it's why people go to school in the first place. Maybe it is my bias as an English teacher, but my impression is that the whole reason people learn anything is so that they can use this information to give them things to write about, and, indeed, the keystone role of publication across all academic disciplines provides objective support for this supposition. Writing is the lingua franca of academic communication, and it plays a similar role in any profession, whether in the form of business plans, legislation, press releases, contracts, presentations, annual reports, performance evaluations, incident reports, social media content and promotional materials, lesson plans, emails, or some other genre. In all these cases, effective writing begins with a sense of personal engagement.

The good news is that this sense of engagement is universally accessible. Everybody cares about something. Human life is organized around nodes of passionate involvement. We care most fervently about ourselves and the immediate people and places that directly touch our lives—our family members and friends, our neighbors and neighborhoods, our hobbies and pastimes. And these passionate centers branch out in many directions, or, rather, they draw into themselves other things—ideas, points of view, histories, mythologies—that become meaningful as ways of understanding the things and people we love. In this way, the entire universe of human reality is woven together through bonds of love, which also become bonds of curiosity, purpose, and meaning-making. The act of writing can be thought of as a process of mapping out these nodes, locating the synaptic connections between them, and even generating new nodes and new connections within this cognitive-cultural architecture. This is why the best, most meaningful writing tends to begin with, as writing teachers often advise their students, "writing what you know" (addressing a topic that is close to home and personally relevant) and then "following the heart" (exploring the paths that branch outward from this emotional center).

UDL emphasizes the importance of providing students with multiple opportunities for establishing and sustaining a level of engagement with their learning, as well as for developing self-awareness regarding their degree of psychological involvement in their academic pursuits. While all students become more adept learners when they feel more engaged in their education, they may vary widely in terms of what kinds of topics engage them, as well as in terms of what kinds of strategies work to get them involved and keep them focused. A UDL-informed approach to designing writing assignments begins with this principle of learner variability, empowering students to find a way into a writing project that works for them. Writing is an extremely personal kind of intellectual activity, meaning that the more closely a student identifies with the goals of a writing project, the more likely they are to "bring their best selves" to the work. The UDL Guidelines provide criteria for enhancing students' opportunities for accessing, building, and internalizing a sense of engagement with their learning, and these criteria can stimulate writing instructors to design writing projects that allow different kinds of student writers to achieve these common goals.

Access to Engagement

The most obvious way to encourage students to develop a personal connection to a writing assignment is to give them the opportunity to determine what they write about. In a class devoted principally to composition, where the foremost goal of the course is to promote students' ability to express themselves in writing and absent any other "content," UDL principles would suggest that more learners can feel more included if the writing topic is as open-ended as possible. While, for academic purposes, the genre in which students are expected to express themselves is likely to be some variation on the research paper, authentic and original research can be conducted around literally any element of human reality. If the goal of the class is to provide a setting where students are likely to discover a personal connection with the act of writing, this goal is most likely to be met by encouraging students to think about what they "research" in their spare time, whether it's basketball statistics, celebrity gossip, hip-hop, or any other cultural phenomenon. Students may be surprised to learn that professional writers develop entire careers writing about these subjects. Moreover, the personal connections students have with their own hobbies and interests give them unique insight that can become the basis for fruitful academic inquiry. Composition instructors who provide predetermined writing topics may unintentionally create barriers for some students who don't connect for whatever reason with the assignment.

Of course, there are also composition classes where the content is relevant to the course goal, such as writing classes in other disciplines. Even if it is crucial, however, that a student writer write about, say, the Russian Revolution, gene editing, or *Plessy v. Ferguson*, UDL-oriented writing instructors support student variability by providing multiple options for students to connect with such preestablished topics. Each of these topics, and any other topic that you can think of, suggests a wide variety of ways into it, including first-person narratives, statistical data, physical artifacts and visual representations, historical perspectives, primary documents, artistic representations, and other forms of writing. Exposing students to different ways of understanding and writing about a shared topic enhances the likelihood that every student will find something that speaks to their personal way of making sense of the world. In some kinds of classes (again, depending on the course goals), the students may be able to express their understanding of the common topic in a genre of writing of their choice, whether it's a poem, a short story, a personal reflection, or a screenplay.

Even if the course goals dictate that the student must produce a research paper about a specific topic, however, students can always be encouraged to spin any writing assignment in a way that helps to align it with their own personality or point of view. Students writing about wilderness conservation might focus on species or spaces that they feel a particular affinity for. Students writing about a historical event can address it from the perspective of what it means (or doesn't mean) to them, and why. Students assessing arguments about social issues can consider the way these issues impact their own neighborhoods, families, and schools. Indeed, the importance of forging this kind of relationship between the goals of a writing project and a writer's own personal goals might be the biggest lesson any writer can learn.

Building Engagement

Writing assignments in composition-oriented classes tend to be spread out over several weeks, involving various "process" stages of brainstorming, researching, outlining, drafting, and revising. This prolonged schedule is conducive to scaffolding and supporting student writing, but it also means that student engagement needs to be sustained—and, ideally, enhanced—over the course of the composition timeline. In addition to striking an initial spark of engagement, a writing project must fuel this spark so that it can grow into an enduring flame.

The writing process is typically imagined as a linear track moving from point A to B to C to D, with all the students following along like railcars. A more UDL-informed model of the writing process, however, might be a plate of spaghetti, where every strand starts off in one place and ends somewhere else, but each finds its own squiggly path. This is particularly important when students are writing about topics that they have chosen themselves; it may be necessary for student writers to experiment with different ways of thinking about the topic in order to tease out how they think and feel about it. In classroom practice, this may mean providing a buffet of options that students can choose as their process work leading up to a writing project. In this context, *process assignments* include any writing students do that is not intended to represent the students' "final word" on anything—these are the compositional equivalents of practicing for a game, rehearsing for a show, experimenting, wandering, and playing. Whereas *product assignments* challenge students to zero in on a definitive way of saying something, process assignments use writing to elaborate ideas, expand perspectives, and open up new ways of thinking and communicating.

Even when the goal of the process is a formal academic paper, students may be able to think through their ideas and internalize the new information they are learning through personal reflection essays, songs and poetry, speculative storytelling, an infographic, a vlog diary, a multimedia journal, or other forms of expression. Students might even be encouraged to choose three process projects from a menu of options as a way of enriching and integrating their understanding of their research topic. The assessment of the writing assignment might be weighted to value these process assignments as equivalent to the final version of the research paper in a way that rewards students for demonstrating creativity, versatility, expansiveness, and curiosity.

For many students, as well as for many writers, the most powerful source of motivation comes from other people. Although there is a stereotype of researching and writing as a lonely experience, it is fundamentally social at every level. Obviously, the whole point of academic writing is to communicate something to other people, and all academic knowledge is built out of relationships among different researchers responding to one another's perspectives and points of view all the way back through history. When writers think of themselves as part of a wider community, they achieve a sense of purpose and interactivity that energizes the writing process, deepens thinking, and sustains motivation. Sometimes, a class of writing students can come together in a way that creates this sense of social engagement, but some students might not click with this group dynamic in the same way. I find it helpful to encourage each individual student to identify their own "research community" composed of friends (inside or outside the class), interview subjects, other teachers, and anyone else they can talk to about their writing project. In the same way that someone is more likely to quit smoking if they tell other people that they are doing it, talking about a writing project with other people can help make it feel more real and more closely aligned with one's personal and social identity.

Internalizing Engagement

Like any other academic task, a writing assignment is never an end in itself. The goal of writing is always to unlock ideas within oneself, to take a step forward into a wider and more complex world, and to raise new questions that require further inquiry and more writing. For this reason, even a well-written student paper is only successful insofar as the student has internalized a personal connection, not only with the content that they're writing about, but also—and more importantly— with their own abilities to use their perspective and their language to map out the world and create meaning. For this reason, student writers benefit from activities that encourage them to reflect on the relationship between their work on a particular writing project and the wider themes and issues that inform their lives.

A research journal—a series of reflective entries that a student compiles as they work on a writing project—can sustain and internalize engagement by helping students foster insight into what they have learned, how the new information connects to what they already know, what they still want to learn, and how their research process is influencing their evolving ideas about the topic. In addition to giving students a space to reflect on their personal relationship with what they're learning, a research journal can also be a place where ideas come together, resulting in new discoveries about both their research topic and about the processes of learning and writing themselves. Student writers can use their research journals to address "meta" concerns related to their writing projects, such as their confidence level, their anxieties, their doubts, and their expectations. Compiling a learning journal can be a chance for students to develop an awareness that writing is just as much (or probably more) about addressing these psychological issues as it is about content or style.

While the act of journaling one's ideas in the form of complete sentences can be a uniquely effective way of cultivating reflective insight, it is important to consider that different students might find it easier and more productive to express themselves in different media as well. As with other process work, a learning journal might take digital, graphic, musical, or multimedia form. Any form of expression that stimulates students to think through the quality of their research journey should be promoted and celebrated.

Representation

In content-based classes, the UDL category of representation refers primarily to the course materials—the manner in which the content is represented to the students. It is certainly important to think about how this kind of content—the "what" of learning—can be provided in multiple ways that optimize accessibility for all students. A lot of UDL practice focuses on representing course content for students through a variety of modalities and formats, but this aspect is less relevant in the composition classroom, where the emphasis is on developing a skill rather than on understanding content. This emphasis may mean that composition instructors downplay in both specific and general ways the extent to which they represent information about writing to their students. I discuss some of the specific ways that writing teachers represent information to their students later in this chapter, but it is also important to pause to consider on a macro scale how writing classes represent the act of writing itself.

In the daily grind of preparing for classes, grading assignments, and managing students, it can be easy to lose sight of the big picture: What does the composition class as a whole teach students about the kind of activity that writing is?

★ Is writing extrinsically or intrinsically motivated?

★ Is writing a linear or nonlinear process?

★ What are the standards of excellence that writers should aspire to?

When we think about these questions, the obvious next step is to try to answer them for ourselves. In the process of doing so, we discover that the answer is always nonbinary. Writing inevitably takes place along a continuum of external and internal motivations—it can even be defined as the project of creating a bridge between one's own motivations and the external structure of the writing situation. Likewise, writers pursue a variety of strategies over the course of their creative process, some of which are linear, as in the mere act of stringing together strands of words and sentences and paragraphs, and some of which are nonlinear, as in the recursive process of revision, the winding path of research, or the unpredictable "lightning effects" that characterize the brainstorming process. When writers consider their own criteria for success, they inevitably find themselves balancing the expectations of the writing situation—which are always variable—with expectations that come entirely from themselves, and which are therefore always evolving and emergent. Writers write for an audience at the same time as they write for themselves, and even against themselves. The point is that writing is a lot of different things in different situations for different people at different times. In fact, it is not an exaggeration to say that writing is never the same thing from one instance to the next—that every time a writer sits down to write, they are a different writer, faced with a different task under different circumstances.

For all of these reasons, one of the most important lessons that writing teachers can teach their students is that writing itself is a multifaceted activity that makes use of all of these different perspectives in various ways. Writing is not one thing; its purpose and its essence is to mobilize the whole person in all of their complexity. Multiply that complexity by the equally infinite complexity of a given writing situation, and multiply that yet again by the infinite complexity of the topic the writer is writing about, and it is easy to understand why writing teachers are tempted to narrow down the writing situation to more manageable parameters, instructing students to write about topic x in style y according to timeline z. And, indeed, narrow parameters are one of the conditions under which skillful writers need to learn to operate. But in order to represent the full scope of what writing can do, it is also worthwhile to represent writing to students in a way that celebrates the diversity of its forms. The concept of the writing process has been an important mainstay of composition studies, but it may be helpful to imagine ways that we can encourage students to think about writing *processes*, plural, that can be applied, modified, and repurposed for different situations.

Because writing is so multifaceted, there are many ways to teach it, each appropriate to the dispositions of and interrelationships between the instructor, the students, and the learning context. The one principle that all writing instruction should foreground, however, is the fact of the universal accessibility of writing, its democratic feature of being able to give a voice to anyone and to any idea. There are many ways that writing instructors can represent the act of writing as an open frontier of human possibilities, but the most meaningful strategy is to model respect for the variety of ways in which students express themselves both in their writing and in other modalities. When writing teachers engineer writing situations that allow students to explore their own voices and follow their own creative pathways, they represent the act of writing as an authentic mode of self-becoming and a celebration of human variability.

Content-Oriented Instruction

While composition is a skills-oriented style of instruction, writing classes typically do present instructional content in one form or another to students, whether it involves information about formatting citations, descriptions of research methodology, or lessons in grammar, vocabulary, and usage. Recent research has suggested that explicit instruction in technical aspects of writing benefits students, but the best way of reaching the most students is to provide various ways to access this kind of information. In a writing class, this means not only supplementing online tutorials with in-person instruction, but also encouraging students to consider aspects of technical usage, citation format, or other elements in their own writing, in the writing of their classmates, and also in that of their instructor and of other writers. Students should have opportunities to listen to formal academic prose in addition to reading it.

It can also be worthwhile for student writers to record themselves reading their own writing, by themselves or for an audience, and listen to it as a way of deepening their self-awareness of how they use language. These kinds of recordings can be developed into podcasts or become the voice-over for narrated slideshows or montage videos. In addition to its conceptual elements, writing has an unavoidably aural quality. Writing with good grammar may have more to do with honing an ear for a certain kind of language than it does with internalizing abstract rules, and this aspect of writing lends particular urgency to the UDL Guidelines that recommend providing students with both auditory and visual options for perceiving educational content.

The technical vocabulary involved in explaining grammatical concepts can be particularly daunting for some students, as well as for many teachers. One way to discuss specific aspects of grammar and usage such as parts of speech, verb tenses, the passive and active voice, and other technical concepts is to begin by asking the students to describe what they know about these topics. In addition to clarifying for the instructor what the students already know, asking the students to start the conversation allows them to assess their own level of comprehension. The instructor might encourage the students to share what they know using whatever media make the most sense to them, developing their own instructional materials in the form of YouTube videos, infographics, worksheets, or in-class presentations. I have found that this kind of lesson empowers students to discover their own answers, and it allows them to communicate their discoveries to their peers in a variety of styles that not only provide numerous options of perception but also frequently speak to their fellow students in ways that instructor-generated content might not. Working on a project like this, students find themselves using the very grammatical structures and technical information that they are explaining, learning something in two ways—conceptually and performatively—at the same time.

Texts: Readings, Research Sources, and Models of Composition

While the most salient goal of composition classes involves the development of students' ability to express themselves in writing, these classes also tend to foreground the importance of deciphering and responding to texts written by other people. Indeed, composition classes are often the only environment in which higher-level students specifically study reading skills and strategies. Writing assignments tend to invite students to "write back" to texts, they often ask students to use information from texts to develop their own arguments, and they are often presented with samples of writing that students are encouraged to emulate. Students vary widely in their reading skills, however, and whenever a class in any discipline presents students with textual information, the UDL Guidelines encourage instructors to consider strategies for enhancing access to the information contained in those texts.

Many writing instructors organize their curriculum around writing assignments tied to a specific reading or set of readings. Students may read an essay by a famous writer and then develop an essay that expands on, applies, rejects, or otherwise comments on the perspective articulated by the famous writer. The easiest way to make such a reading more accessible is by providing it in an audio or audiovisual format. If an audio or audiovisual version of the text is not available, student groups might be assigned the task of producing one. Such an assignment not only allows the students to produce more accessible versions of the texts, but also encourages them to attend carefully to the structure and style of the text itself. If the text includes a challenging vocabulary of allusions, students can also work together to pool their background knowledge, conduct research, and develop a glossary of terms and references in order to help one another decode it.

In addition to trying to open up the text to multiple media, however, instructors might consider whether a single authoritative text is necessary in order to reach the goals of the class. Indeed, the skill of careful and critical reading is an invaluable subskill in the practice of effective writing, but if the goal is simply to get students to think and to write, a more robust portfolio of rhetorical stimuli—documentaries, podcasts, news footage, photographs, and so on—may be just as effective at evoking responses from students. I would also argue that, whenever possible, it is best practice to give students a voice in the topics and texts they are required to write about. When students have a say in what they read and write about in a composition class, not only is their work more likely to be authentic and meaningful, but texts and topics are more likely to represent the world the students come from and the concerns that preoccupy them.

When composition students conduct research for their writing projects, they are typically directed toward written texts. Many composition students are encouraged to believe that the only reliable source of information is academic articles from scholarly journals. Articles from scholarly journals are notoriously difficult to understand, even for professionals in scholarly disciplines, and they tend to be written in a style that exacerbates this obscurity. For students, this must communicate the message that the only reliable source is one that is maddeningly opaque, and that they are doomed to be stranded in the wilderness of epistemological chaos. Of course, while academic articles from scholarly journals can provide useful information, it would be the height of ivory tower elitism to deny that they are merely one—and a kind of esoteric one, at that—source of human wisdom and authority.

Moreover, while it is possible to build interesting ideas by recombining the ideas articulated by other academicians in other academic journals, it is undeniably more interesting, more original, and more productive to consider a research process that examines a wide variety of perspectives regarding the research topic. Again, if one of the goals of a writing class is helping students develop their ability to read scholarly articles, then activities that help scaffold and interpret these texts are likely to enhance this goal for all students. If the goal is simply to get students to think and to write, however, a research process is more likely to involve them and leverage their unique skills if it also encompasses other forms of "data," such as personal interviews and conversations, popular press articles, polling results, social media posts, primary sources, documentary footage, and other kinds of input. As part of their writing process, students should present their research data to one another as their research process unfolds, allowing them to share perspectives and insights and to articulate critical questions and interpretations.

Another important role that written texts play in composition classes is to serve as models for a student's own writing. Seeing how another student responded to a certain writing project provides students with helpful examples of how to format and develop their own writing, and it communicates the impression that the writing project is achievable. As with these other kinds of texts, however, it is important to make these sample texts accessible, not only to help readers who may experience specific challenges with decoding texts, but also to make clear the model properties of the sample essay for all students. A class activity that encourages students to annotate a sample essay with notes about its strengths and weaknesses allows students to create a meta-textual scaffold that clarifies the lessons that the sample essay has to teach. As with other kinds of decoding activities, this scaffold might involve in-class conversations, audiovisual responses to specific aspects, graphic outlines or organizers that analyze the rhetorical structure of the sample essay, and other ways of representing the information that the essay contains (in its structure and style as well as in its content). Activities that ask students to dig into texts, to paraphrase them in their own words, and to represent them in other formats not only make this textual information more available to more students, but also allow students to perform reading strategies that enhance their overall literacy and their self-efficacy as readers.

Feedback to Student Writers

Because writing is an inherently social activity, the loop of writing is never complete until writers get a chance to discover how readers respond to what they have written. In authentic writing situations, this feedback typically comes from diverse audiences, and it may take various forms and respond to different elements and levels of the piece of writing under consideration. The best way for composition instructors to ensure that their students receive robust, meaningful, and constructive responses to their writing is to provide multiple opportunities for multiple audiences to respond in multiple ways to what the student has written, and then to give the student opportunities to "talk back" to these responses. As any writer discovers, this kind of give-and-take can help writers see their own work from other perspectives and become more self-aware about how the choices they make influence the way their writing is perceived and interpreted. Replicating this experience in the classroom requires composition instructors to integrate opportunities for students to receive this kind of feedback into the writing process, rather than merely tacking them on as an afterthought or post-hoc exercise. In a classroom, the most valuable sort of feedback comes from the student writers themselves, the other students in the class, and the instructor, and the UDL Guidelines can help ensure that each source of feedback is accessible and useful to the student writer.

Before anyone else responds to a piece of student writing, it is advisable to allow the students themselves to assess their own writing. Doing so allows the student writer to switch hats from writer to reader, while also activating the kind of background knowledge that can help the writer work through their own ideas about what came out well and what could be further improved in the piece. Students can be encouraged to annotate their own essays with questions and observations about what they've written, and instructors can develop these reflections further by encouraging students to write or record reviews of their own writing to share with their classmates. These reviews can become a starting point for class discussions, which can replicate the multidimensional aspect of how communities respond to texts. Students responding to each other's writing should always be coached to emphasize positive commentary on the substance of what the writer has set out to say, rather than harping on specific errors or shortcomings. This kind of strengths-based peer assessment can help the student writer identify the most promising elements of their writing and build on their success. In addition to open-ended classroom discussion, peer assessments can also take the form of live or recorded interviews with the student writer, multimedia reviews, and illustrations or outlines that highlight key aspects of the student's work.

Of course, the instructor also has an important role to play in this conversation. While it may be helpful for the instructor to edit student writing in a way that points out deviations from standard technical usage, this kind of sentence-level feedback should always be contextualized within the wider framework of what the student has been trying to do in a piece of writing and what kinds of audiences the student is trying to reach. Writing is extremely personal, and critiques of a student's writing can often feel to a student like a critique of their intellect, culture, and identity. Taking a broader approach, one that begins with the purpose and audience being addressed, helps clarify for the student that suggested revisions advance their own purposes—that the edits are pragmatic rather than judgmental in nature and intended to amplify the student's voice, not squelch it.

Providing multifaceted feedback that considers various aspects of the student writing in multiple modalities also helps situate specific grammatical feedback within a wider context. Therefore, in addition to sentence-level editorial feedback, instructor responses to student writing should address the general scope of what the writer has set out to do. Rather than comparing a student's writing to some abstract model of standard prose, students and instructors can work together to identify how effectively the student's draft realizes the goals that the student started off with. When students have a voice in establishing their own expectations, analysis of their drafts is framed in terms of their progress toward their goals—a progress that may also involve articulating increasingly ambitious goals as they work through their writing process—rather than being framed in terms of the students' failure to meet educational goals articulated in advance by teachers, traditions, and problematic cultural histories.

In a writing class, it may seem to make sense to conduct these discussions through the medium of writing, but one-on-one conferences and small-group discussions allow students to ask questions about comments or edits that have been marked on their drafts, while also making the feedback process feel more bidirectional and participatory. Most impactfully, students should have opportunities to respond to the instructor's feedback—to supply their own feedback on the feedback—in the form of a revision journal, a video or audio reflection, or an outline detailing their ideas about how they want to use the feedback they have received. This kind of activity not only helps the students process this feedback but also allows the instructor to get a sense of how it has been received. When students compose their own responses to their readers, they take back ownership of their writing and assert their own participation in the important work of using feedback to strengthen their self-efficacy as writers.

Action and Expression

Something magical happens when a person starts writing. The whole brain erupts into activity, from the sensorimotor areas that control the typing fingers, to the short-term memory circuits that hold a framework for the sentence in mind as it is being constructed, to the linguistic memory to supply vocabulary and grammatical forms. Writing combines the social-emotional work of identifying the appropriate tone, the introspective work of identifying psychologically with the sentence as it takes shape, and the deeply personal and philosophical work of articulating one's own underlying belief systems. Writing—in any style or genre—is an expression of a writer's entire selfhood. The teaching of writing, therefore, is inescapably a process of encouraging learners to channel their own selfhood—to develop a richer understanding of themselves, to express themselves more faithfully, and to challenge themselves to be themselves more fully.

Everyone who writes does so with their own words, in their own voice, from their own unique perspective. Even when writers are trying to write like someone else, the psycholinguistic dynamics of writing make it inevitably, almost alarmingly, self-revealing. Writing teachers know that every student has a unique way of using language to express themselves—that no two students use the same word in exactly the same way, and that no two students will ever write exactly the same sentence. Writing teachers know that the goal of writing education is not to get all their students to write the same thing, or even to write the same way, but to write in ways that authentically express their unique style of seeing the world. Writing teachers also know that this linguistic and cognitive diversity is central to the whole "project" of writing, which is to amplify and celebrate the variety of human experience. For these reasons, people who teach writing tend to sympathize with the founding premise of Universal Design for Learning: that learner variability is an inevitable condition of all educational settings.

As previously mentioned, this book is primarily inspired by the question of how to apply UDL principles in ways that retain a focus on writing in the traditional sense. Encouraging writing students to experiment with the diverse forms of communication available in today's world is certainly worthwhile and can stimulate new ideas and approaches. The action of expressing oneself in written words and sentences, however, has cognitive and intellectual value that differentiates it from other modes of expression. As a strategy of knowledge transformation, the intellectual labor involved in translating personal ideas into specific, intentionally crafted words and sentences facilitates a higher level of neurological integration of new ideas with old ones, forging a personal connection between subject matter and learner and establishing a foundation for advanced and complex inquiry. I do not mean to imply that composing in other media does not have its own cognitive values, but text-based writing has always held a privileged position in the ecosystem of expressive media, and we do students a disservice if we deprive them of opportunities to develop this critical cognitive and communicative skill. In any event, as K–12 teachers know, writing fluently is one of the core competencies that their students are expected to master, and, as college-level writing teachers know, effective writing is one of the most valuable skills that their students will need to succeed in their careers. The question, therefore, is not *whether* we should teach "writing" in the old-fashioned sense, but *how* we can do it in a way that acknowledges the fact that different students might need different systems of support to develop their writing skills.

Physical Action

Although we typically think of writing as an intellectual activity, it also has a physical aspect that can present challenges for certain learners. In addition to the complex motor skills of handwriting and typing, the requirement that writers typically sit in one place for long periods of time can also present obstacles to success that have nothing to do with the quality of the students' ideas or their ability to compose meaningful sentences. Writing teachers should familiarize themselves with various assistive technologies that can reduce some of these barriers, not only because they can help students who identify as having special needs, but also because other students may find these tools helpful for many of the same reasons.

Pencil grips and slant boards can make it easier for some students to write by hand, while a host of assistive technologies can make it easier for students to write at a keyboard or to render their handwritten compositions into digital form. Ergonomic keyboards, keyboards with enlarged keys, high-contrast keyboards, and braille keyboards can be invaluable resources for students with specific accommodations, but it is also likely that making some of these other formats available, especially for students at any level who are just beginning to learn to type, could make the physical work of typing less onerous. Likewise, key guards, palm pads, and finger rests alleviate some of the physical strain of typing, lowering a significant but often neglected barrier to writing. While some of this equipment is expensive, on-screen keyboards can be easily reconfigured into different formats and can also be accessed by mouse, switch, or eye gaze.

In addition to the ubiquitous spell-check and grammar-check utilities, some students also find the word prediction tool to be a helpful guide that enables them to find their way to the next part of a sentence. Speech-to-text is one of the most useful technological tools my students have used to help them compose assignments in a way that bypasses the physical demands of typing. Student writers can write out their thoughts in longhand and then read their composition into a speech-to-text program; outline their composition and then improvise their way through the sentences; or extemporize the whole piece. In any event, their composition is rendered in digital, textual form, which they can then go on to edit or revise as needed. Likewise, the text-to-speech function, by allowing students to hear their own sentences read back to them, may make it easier for them to detect elements of their writing that they want to revise.

In addition to the physical demands of handwriting and typing, composition also places demands on a writer's ability to focus and concentrate, while also taxing a writer's working memory. "Set and setting" play a huge role in how much of an obstacle it is to activate and sustain a writer's attention. Student writers should be encouraged to find a physical setting that is free of distractions and where they feel comfortable. Inevitably, certain students will find it harder to find such a space than others. If finding a "room of their own" to write in is a challenge, this obstacle needs to be addressed explicitly, since it is impossible for anyone to do anything if there is nowhere for them to do it. Writing instructors can make time available during class for students to write, or they can arrange with the school library and administration to make space available outside of class hours. Students should be encouraged to try writing in different environments to find a place that works for them, as well as to experiment with various routines or rituals that help them get into the writing zone. Again, having an explicit conversation about where and under what conditions students write best can help the instructor and student identify and examine logistical obstacles and work together to find solutions.

Likewise, different students will likely find different writing schedules more motivational than others. While some students may prefer to sit down for an hour to write a complete composition, other students may find it easier to break the task into two 30-minute shifts, or even four 15-minute shifts spread out over a few days. The nature of writing fortunately allows for this kind of flexibility, and part of learning to write involves discovering the rhythms that fit with your personal habits of mind.

Students can also expand their understanding of their ideal writing situation by writing in different social environments. While solitude is generally considered the default social environment for writers, some student writers may find the sustained isolation disquieting and itself a distraction. All students can benefit from the experience of writing alongside the instructor or a tutor, or even working with a scribe. Similarly, writing in small groups with other classmates not only can help student writers who feel more comfortable working in others' company, but also can increase any writer's awareness of how different environments influence the way they write.

Expression and Communication

Students preparing to participate in the contemporary information ecosystem benefit from learning to express themselves across a wide range of platforms and formats. Even in a classroom where the instructional outcomes focus on students' textual writing skills, however, it is worthwhile to consider the way that so-called traditional writing intersects with other modes of self-expression, and the ways that thinking about multimodality can enhance the relevance and impact of writing projects. Academicians writing a book typically represent the information in the book in the form of a conference presentation, a research poster, a blog post, a radio interview, a series of tweets, a YouTube video, a recorded interview, a talk show appearance, and possibly many other media, often at the same time that they are writing the book. Professional authors develop their books into documentaries, TED Talks, infomercials, pilot episodes for streaming series, audiobooks, and other forms of representation. An author's work on these alternative modes of discourse often influences the way their thinking and their writing evolves, adding complexity and perspective to the author's ideas. Moreover, the proliferation of these other media tends to underscore the importance and uniqueness of the writing itself as their foundation—as the most definitive expression of the author's ideas. For students raised in a densely multimedia environment, the value of writing well may become easier to appreciate when their text becomes the script for a narrated video or a podcast. Rather than replacing traditional writing instruction with instruction in other media, a multimedia approach to composition can enhance composition instruction for all students by demonstrating the important role that writing plays in the development of any other form of media.

The process of writing out a draft—the part of the proverbial writing process where the actual writing happens—intimidates many students and professional writers alike with the sense that they are stepping into a void, a space without any landmarks or beacons. Inviting students to think about their writing assignments as multimedia projects can help them fill this empty space with recognizable features that guide the writing process through specific "stations." The definitive example of this effect is a lecturer who uses a series of images in a slideshow as reminders of what each part of their talk is supposed to do. Developing a slideshow of sorts for a paper can serve as a visual outline that similarly helps student writers fill out the specific points they want to make as they compose their paragraphs. Students writing about scientific topics sometimes find it helpful to write around specific charts or graphs, developing their composition as a series of interconnected discussions of specific data points. Likewise, students writing about history or the visual arts can include historical photographs or reproductions of artistic images in their writing, both to help them find their way from one paragraph to the next and to give them something very specific and concrete to write about within individual paragraphs.

It also may be helpful for students to have an opportunity to talk through their ideas before they draft out a piece of writing, possibly in the form of a presentation to the class, in an oral overview for the instructor, or in small groups of fellow students. Through these social interactions, students can hear their own ideas and experiment with different ways of expressing them before hammering them out into specific words and sentences. If student writers are encouraged to develop their compositions into narrated videos or slideshows, or into podcasts or audiobooks, they may think more deliberately and self-consciously about how they want to choose their words, and the experience of developing these multimedia materials provides an object lesson in how words on a page can become amplified on a global scale. Writers at any level of proficiency benefit from embracing the multimedia dimensions that are inherent in any expressive act.

Executive Function

The role of executive function has unique importance when it comes to student writing. Most academic assignments, such as taking a test, completing a worksheet, or answering study questions, come with very specific instructions about what is to be done and how. Writing assignments, however, especially longer writing assignments, no matter how scaffolded they are by a process approach and the other UDL-informed supports, ultimately succeed or fail largely on the student writer's ability to set appropriate goals, develop a strategy to meet the goals, and evaluate their own progress as they move along. In addition to these meta-level decisions, student writers need to develop the empowered autonomy that allows them to make the thousands of micro-decisions that go into writing a single paragraph. Making both the meta-level and the micro-level decisions with confidence—on your own, on the fly, in the foggy landscape of an unwritten paragraph—requires an entrepreneurial pluck that is the essence of the personality that comes across when students write in their own voice, as their own boss, on their own conditions. Some students inevitably find it easier than others to develop this sense of ownership of their writing, but all writers can benefit from experimenting with different ways of becoming more reflective about how they make decisions—decisions about the content and language of their writing as well as those about how, where, when, and why they write.

Instructors can facilitate this kind of metacognitive reflection by providing students with opportunities to think through these big questions. I mentioned previously that a writing journal can help students identify and sustain their motivation to complete a particular writing project, but keeping a journal like this over the course of a year or semester across several writing projects can help student writers achieve more comprehensive insight into how they behave as writers, what composition strategies work for them, and how they have learned and grown as writers. This emphasis on reflection is particularly valuable in a UDL-informed learning environment where the instructor provides students with a buffet of options for engagement, representation, and action and expression. Reflective activities can help students arrive at conclusions about which options were the most useful for them and why.

In a writing class, it may seem intuitive to encourage students to conduct these metacognitive reflections through the medium of writing, but the point of this activity is to stimulate thinking rather than to practice writing, and some students find it easier to think freely and creatively when they are talking out loud to themselves, having a conversation with a classmate, or doodling diagrams or illustrations. Some students might find it easier to respond to direct prompts (e.g., "Describe a time when you felt like you were writing well. What do you think it was about that time that allowed you to write well?"), while other students might prefer a more open-ended format. Some students might take a more analytical approach, while others might find that a storytelling approach expresses their experiences more faithfully. Ideally, every student writer should get a chance to think about their writing experiences from all of these different angles and in all of these different contexts. As they examine their writing experiences from these various perspectives, they develop a clearer sense of their own identity as writers, an impression that might look very different from one student to another, but which will be universal in the sense that it is rooted in the democratic principle that all students succeed when they are allowed the chance to express their human uniqueness.

The cultivation of this "universal" uniqueness might even be said to be the most important goal of all writing instruction, and even of education itself. More important than what a student writes or what a student learns is their growing awareness of and appreciation for the power of their own minds to shape information, to craft ways of thinking, and to invent new ideas. The fact that a student writer can start off with nothing and end up—after days or weeks of trial and error, hope and frustration, agony and ecstasy—with a composition, a snapshot of their own thinking available to all other humans for all eternity, serves as striking evidence of their ability to write their own lives, to shape their own future, and to change the world with their ideas. As students come to feel empowered as writers, they write themselves into existence as thoughtful, passionate, articulate participants in a global and pan-historical human conversation.

Part II

Practice: UDL-Informed Writing Activities

Building Community

A writing class is a unique kind of human environment. Like any educational setting, the writing classroom is a space dedicated to discovery and analysis, but rather than directing students' thoughts to curricular content, the "content" of a writing class is the students themselves—their own thoughts and feelings, their anxieties and dreams, their ways of being in the world and of expressing themselves, and even their relationships with one another and with the teacher. While writing students may be researching and writing about content, they are doing so (ideally) in their own words, from their own points of view, and from within the material circumstances of their own lives. And while writing classes often contain their own kind of content—rules of grammar and paragraph construction, reference formats, rhetorical structure, and so on—this information is valuable only to the extent that students use it as a means of articulating their own perspectives. In a time when educators are learning to emphasize the pedagogical importance of social-emotional learning, self-awareness, and interpersonal dialogue, writing classrooms regularly challenge students to investigate their attitudes and biases, to talk through complicated or controversial ideas, and to feel empowered to use their voices with confidence and compassion.

This is difficult work to do, and it requires a team effort on the part of the teacher and the students. The most successful writing classrooms tend to be those that invest energy in developing and sustaining a sense of community. At its best, the writing community of the classroom can become a microcosm of the global community of readers and writers. Just like "real" writers, student writers are motivated by the prospect of communicating what they think and feel to other people. In a supportive and joyful classroom community, students write for one another as much as or more than they write for the teacher. Not only does this community dynamic encourage the students to write more and challenge them to write more effectively, but it also provides a critical lesson in the meaning of writing itself, which is, at its heart, a means of bringing people together and helping them understand one another.

Creating this engaging classroom dynamic begins with the value of inclusivity. Students need to feel that they are actively welcomed into the learning environment and that the learning environment itself has been designed to accommodate them, no matter who they are. UDL-informed pedagogy begins with the recognition that any group of students reflects the diversity of human beings at large. Any course design that doesn't take this diversity into account is certain to exclude some students and, just as damaging to the spirit of the classroom community, telegraph to all the students that some are more welcome than others. When teachers provide students with a variety of means to become engaged in the work of the classroom, they honor the students' uniqueness while also fostering their executive decision-making skills. Creating a nurturing classroom community allows students to hear from multiple perspectives, participate in multiple forms of social interaction, and practice multiple styles of communication. In short, an inclusive classroom leverages the diversity of the students as a powerful teaching opportunity. This dynamic is particularly effective in the writing classroom, where the diversity of human voices both challenges students to communicate across this diversity while also encouraging students to find and refine their own voice. Inclusive course design ensures that every student has a chance to be part of the conversation.

The activities in this section of the book are intended to promote a sense of community among the students by giving them an opportunity to get to know one another, to teach one another writing skills, and to define their own identity as writers. While all of these assignments involve writing in a variety of ways, they also give students opportunities to work with other media and to express themselves through nontextual means. The activities allow students to work in various social configurations, as well as by themselves, and they foreground the students' individual experiences as human beings and their authority as writers and speakers. These kinds of community-building projects welcome all students to reflect on who they are and what they have to say, and they foster a safe space where these conversations can take place in an atmosphere of respect, open-mindedness, and inclusivity.

Icebreaker Profile

In any classroom environment, the most important first step is developing a sense of mutual recognition and trust among the participants. This activity helps students learn about one another, while also providing a dramatic lesson in the process of translating direct experience into written words. It also has the benefit of introducing students to the writing process: collecting information, organizing it into a sequence, expressing this sequence of information in sentences and paragraphs, and responding to feedback to enhance the accuracy and impact of their writing.

 UDL Overview

While the outcome of this activity is a conventional written profile essay, the students are encouraged to use multiple media as a means of both expressing themselves and understanding their interview partners. The activity also involves a demonstration from the instructor to model the executive functions involved in the assignment, as well as multiple opportunities for students to identify obstacles and receive support from the teacher and from one another.

GOAL:

Provide students with opportunities to engage with one another, with the classroom environment, and with the writing process.

YOU WILL NEED:

- ★ multimedia artifacts to introduce yourself to the class
- ★ a website or learning management system (LMS) for hosting student profile essays and peer responses

TIME:

Four or five class sessions

OUTCOMES:

Students will:

- ★ brainstorm interview questions for a profile essay
- ★ use multimedia artifacts to express their inner lives
- ★ conduct personal interviews and record subjects' responses
- ★ interpret and organize personal artifacts and interview notes
- ★ draft profile essays
- ★ respond to their classmates' representation of them with editorial feedback
- ★ collaborate with interview subjects in a revision process
- ★ prepare their profile essays for digital publication
- ★ respond to profile essays with critical questions
- ★ discuss and reflect on their writing experience

> **UDL Insight**
>
> In such a personal assignment, it is particularly important to allow students a wide range of options for which "artifacts" they want to choose to represent themselves. Some students are likely to be more comfortable talking about themselves than others, so providing multiple options allows students to decide how personal they want to get. At the same time, basing this assignment around a multimedia artifact provides multiple points of engagement with the activity, for both the students presenting their artifact and the student writing the profile.

DIRECTIONS:

1. Ask students to identify personal artifacts, media, or other items that express their personal identities or that mean something special to them. It might be helpful to devote some time to brainstorming the kinds of items that they might consider. These may include:

   ★ personal photographs or videos of their friends or families

   ★ cards, emails, or social media posts that have personal significance

   ★ favorite songs, movies, or online videos

   ★ a favorite memento, piece of clothing, or souvenir

   The more choices they have of how to define this question, the more likely they are to choose something original and meaningful. Students may choose two or three items to bring into class and may also write a brief paragraph explaining their choices.

2. On the day that the students bring in their personal items, present an item that represents something important about your own

personality. In discussion with the class, model the process of explaining how the item expresses your own inner life. Consider:

★ the story behind your connection with the object

★ details of the object that are particularly important or meaningful to you

★ associations, memories, or feelings that the object evokes for you

Encourage the students to ask you questions about your relationship with the artifact and to take notes on what you say.

As a class, sketch out a draft of a short profile essay that uses the artifact as a starting point for introducing the teacher.

 AI Aside

If students are looking for examples of other profile essays to use as a model for their own writing, there are obviously many to choose from that are readily available online. But it is also an interesting experience to ask a chatbot to write a profile of some public figure whom the students might already know something about. Seeing the profile essay that a chatbot composes about, say, Oprah Winfrey not only produces a passable example of what a profile essay might look like, but also provides an opportunity to observe the features of a profile essay that the chatbot is emulating, from the way the essay begins to the structure of the essay itself to the way the chatbot frames the concluding paragraph. Analyzing the chatbot essay allows students a chance to reverse-engineer it, identifying the "rules" that the chatbot is following. They can then apply the same formula to their own writing. This analysis can also reveal the limitations of the chatbot's writing style, particularly its overreliance on the rote formula that it's following.

3. Now it's the students' turn to share their artifacts with one another. Divide the students into pairs. First, one student will present their artifact to their partner. The partner should follow the process modeled during the whole-class activity, asking questions and taking notes. Then the partners can switch roles so that the interviewer becomes the interviewee and vice versa. Students should come away from this interview with sufficient information to begin writing their own artifact-based profile essay.

It can be helpful to provide students with a project overview, which may look something like this:

ONLINE CLASSMATE PROFILE ESSAY OVERVIEW AND INSTRUCTIONS

Who are you? What do you love? What is important to you? If you could only save one possession, what would it be and why? What's your favorite photograph, your favorite article of clothing, your favorite song?

Thinking about these questions can be a powerful opportunity for us to reflect on where we've been and where we're going. These reflections empower us to understand ourselves more fully and to express ourselves more confidently.

In this writing project, we'll begin by identifying an important "artifact" that expresses something important about ourselves. You will work with a partner to describe the significance of your object, while your partner describes the importance of their object to you, and then you will each write short essays about your partner based on these interviews.

The goal of this activity is to help us get to know one another, and help us get to know ourselves as well. It will also give us a chance to consider how writing can be a tool for expressing what we know about ourselves and about one another, and for sharing this knowledge with a wider community.

This assignment involves the following steps:

1. Identify your personal artifact.
2. Work with a partner to learn about each other.
3. Write a profile essay about your partner.
4. Revise your profile essay and prepare it for digital publication.
5. Answer classmates' questions about both the profile essay that you have written and the profile essay that your partner has written about you.

While the student pairs should be encouraged to work autonomously, it is important for you as the teacher to be actively present. Pairs of students often need a little encouragement to help get their process started, especially in the first few weeks of class. The circulating presence of the teacher also helps keep students on task and reinforces the sense that you are accessible. In this activity, students will find it helpful if you can suggest strategies for developing their interview notes into ideas for sentences and paragraphs.

 Composition Connection

Giving interview subjects a chance to review the profile essay that has been written about them provides a lesson in the ethics of writing. It reinforces the responsibility that writers have to respect the people they write about and to commit themselves to truthfulness and accuracy in their writing.

4. After drafting their profile essays, the profile partners reconvene to read each other's drafts. While reading an essay written about

themselves, each partner should consider whether they feel they have been accurately represented. This discussion can be an opportunity for students to fact-check their partner's statements, to highlight instances where their partner wrote something perceptive and insightful, and possibly to locate instances where their partner's writing could be revised in ways that make the profile essay more truthful.

Profile partners should each come away from this second interview with specific revision instructions for ensuring that the representation of their partner presented in the profile essay is one that their partner will endorse.

5. Prepare the revised profile essay for digital publication. After confirming that the revised version of the essay is acceptable to the profile subjects, consult with the student teams, offering additional editorial feedback. A final revision of the profile essay should be accompanied by a photo, digital copy, or link that provides access to the profile subject's artifact, and a photo of the profile subject themselves may also be incorporated into the document.

6. Post the finished profile essays to a website or to the discussion board of the class's LMS so that all students have access to one another's work.

7. Randomly assign students to read three of their classmates' profile essays. For each essay they read, they should respond with two questions: one question for the subject of the profile essay, and one for the writer of the profile essay.

8. These questions can then become the starting point for a talk show–style class activity, where subject/writer pairs take the stage to answer their classmates' questions about their lives and their work. Inviting students to participate in this kind of exchange celebrates their accomplishment in having completed this activity, while also positioning them as professional writers speaking authoritatively about their craft. The juxtaposition of discussions about the

students' lives and about their experience as writers presents opportunities to reflect on how personal the act of writing is.

You can facilitate the discussion in a way that is either wide-ranging and expansive or more tightly focused, depending on the goals of the class. In a composition classroom, this discussion might be a productive opportunity to identify writing topics for future assignments based on the students' interests. Ideally, these conversations can also open out into discussions about the value of writing itself as a tool for exploring ourselves, our worlds, and one another.

ADDITIONAL SUGGESTIONS:

★ In a synchronous online class, student pairs can be assigned to breakout rooms. In an asynchronous online class, student pairs can communicate with each other on the discussion board or via email, and the final "talk show" activity can take place on the discussion board as well.

★ If there is an odd number of students, or if a student prefers to work by themselves, they can choose to either interview someone outside the class (a sibling, mentor, etc.) or write an artifact-based profile of themselves, responding to the "talk show" questions as both subject and author.

DIY Writing Handbook

Should writing teachers provide explicit instruction in aspects of conventional usage? Or should they learn by doing? Why not do both at the same time? This interactive activity invites students to become the experts, compiling their own multimedia writing handbook and sharing their expertise with their fellow students.

UDL Overview

This activity uses multiple means of engagement to invite students into a conversation about basic aspects of writing, and it uses multiple means of action and expression to help students communicate what they know in both writing and through other media. The activity emphasizes students' ability to develop expertise in a particular content area and also to become expert learners.

GOAL:

Engage students in inquiry about technical aspects of the writing process.

YOU WILL NEED:

★ examples of writing handbooks from academic publishers

★ PowerPoint, voice-recording, and other multimedia capabilities

TIME:

Five or six class sessions

OUTCOMES:

Students will:

★ research and report on elements of usage and the writing process

★ draft and revise handbook chapters

★ present their handbook chapter to their classmates using one of several media options

- ★ prepare an assessment activity to gauge reader comprehension
- ★ take student-generated assessments of their comprehension of other students' handbook chapters
- ★ read and respond to other students' handbook chapters
- ★ compile a writing handbook that will be available for them to consult for future writing assignments
- ★ practice graphic layout, expository communication, and multimedia publication

 UDL Insight

Providing students with opportunities to choose their own working conditions optimizes individual choice and autonomy (7.1). Encouraging them to identify their own learning goals optimizes the relevance and authenticity of the project (7.2). Encouraging students to reflect on whether they want to explain something they already know, or to learn about something that they don't know yet, encourages self-assessment and metacognitive reflection (9.3). All these UDL Guidelines fall under the category of strategies for enhancing engagement.

DIRECTIONS:

1. Invite students to examine the examples of online or print-based writing handbooks. If a writing handbook has been assigned as part of the class, they can start with that, but you might bring in a selection of such handbooks from the library or from the faculty bookshelf. You can also have students look for other kinds of tutorials related to writing instruction, such as informational web pages, blog posts, and YouTube videos.

Guiding questions:

★ What kinds of techniques do these sources use to communicate technical information?

★ What sources are most helpful for you personally as a learner?

★ What kinds of commonalities or inconsistencies do you notice from one source to another?

★ How are the handbooks or websites arranged? How do they organize the different kinds of information they cover?

 Composition Connection

Articulating an answer to the learning goal question emphasizes the goal-directed perspective that is an important part of both UDL pedagogy and composition practice. It also serves as an aid to writing and revision, providing students with an objective criterion that can help them compose chapters around the goal and revise their chapter drafts to optimize the extent to which they advance their self-identified goal.

2. Drawing from the examples of topics covered in the sample handbooks, invite students to select a topic that they will cover in their own entry for a student-generated writing handbook. Students may choose to work individually, in pairs, or in small groups. They should also be encouraged to choose to write about either a topic they are already familiar with or one they want to learn more about. They can also choose from a range of more technical aspects of grammar and punctuation (verb agreement, semicolon usage, etc.) and more subjective aspects of the writing process (brainstorming techniques, "finding your voice," etc.).

It can be helpful to provide students with a project overview, which may look something like this:

WRITING TUTORIAL PROJECT OVERVIEW AND INSTRUCTIONS

The world needs our help. People have urgent questions about basic aspects of the writing process, and we can use our expertise to give them information and strategies that will help them succeed. Along the way, we can also teach ourselves and each other about some of the technical and procedural elements of the writing process.

We will be creating narrated PowerPoint videos about specific writing topics. You may choose from among the following suggested topics or propose your own.

colons and semicolons	capitalization
fragments and run-on sentences	commonly confused homophones
commonly misused words	active voice and passive voice
apostrophes	using quotations
writing a body paragraph	writing an introduction
writing a conclusion	articulating a thesis statement
italics	avoiding plagiarism
abbreviations	brainstorming ideas
revision strategies	collaborative writing
time management	coming up with a good title

You are welcome to work with a partner.

Once you have chosen a topic, this assignment involves the following steps:

1. Research your topic. You can use *The Little Seagull Handbook* or any reliable internet-based source. Consult more than one source to make sure that you are getting a robust range of perspectives. Draw up an **outline** of things you plan to discuss in your chapter.
2. Develop your outline into a **chapter** for the handbook. The chapter should be written out in complete sentences and carefully proofread.
3. Develop a **multimedia project** that aligns with your chapter's learning objective.
4. Develop a five-question multiple-choice quiz or other **assessment method** to evaluate your audience's comprehension of your presentation.
5. Present your **chapter** and your **multimedia project** and administer your **assessment**.

3. Encourage students to use a variety of research sources to gather information about their handbook topic. Devote at least one class session or discussion board thread to a conversation in which each student or group of students has an opportunity to describe what they are learning about their topic, where they are finding the most useful information, what (if anything) they are confused about regarding their topic, and how they plan to present this information in their chapter drafts.

As students begin to develop their chapters, they should each compose a brief response to the following learning goal question:

★ What do I want the reader to be able to do after having read my handbook entry?

Facilitate a class discussion in which students and groups share their response to this question.

AI Aside

After students have drafted their own handbook entries, an instructive next step is to ask a chatbot to "write a handbook entry about how to use semicolons" (or similar). How does each student's draft compare with the chatbot essay? Is there anything the chatbot said that they want to include in their own handbook entry (rules they overlooked or suggestions they didn't think of)? What do they like about their own entry that distinguishes it from the chatbot version? This conversation can also open out into a wider consideration of the role that chatbots can play as a writing partner or consultant, especially when it comes to more technical or objective kinds of writing projects.

4. Work with students to develop their notes into outlines and drafts for their handbook entries. Depending on the size of the class and the instructional level, this process can be done either individually by the students for homework or in class in a workshop setting.

   Based on examples from other handbooks, students can follow a basic template for their entries:

   a. Identify and introduce the topic.

   b. List and explain the relevant rules or suggestions.

   c. Provide examples.

   d. Articulate a brief conclusion about the value of this topic.

   Encourage students to consider how they can use images to add impact to their entries. They can also consider how using boldface, italics, or color-coding can help make their example sentences easier to understand.

5. In a class discussion or online discussion board, ask students to brainstorm ideas for an assessment strategy based on their answer to the learning goal question.

   The default assessment strategy might be a multiple-choice quiz posted on Google Docs or some other online site. Depending on their answer to the question, however, some students might consider alternative forms of assessment, such as a brief writing assignment, an error correction activity, open-ended comprehension questions, or anything else that seems appropriate.

6. Invite students to consider how they can use different media to disseminate the information in their handbook chapters. The default approach might be a PowerPoint-based oral presentation, but students might be encouraged to identify different communication strategies based on the nature of their topic and their own expressive preferences. Students may develop narrated PowerPoint videos, vlog- or podcast-style reports, infographics, educational skits, infomercials, or other modes of presentation. Use the learning goal question as a guide to make sure that the multimedia content focuses on the same goal as the textual content.

7. Provide students with an opportunity to share their work with one another.

   ★ **The handbook:** Compile the final drafts of the student chapters into a single document, or the students can assemble this document collaboratively in a shared digital space. Discuss alternatives for organizing the information and indexing the entire document to optimize utility.

   ★ **Multimedia presentations:** Students present their multimedia presentations to the class. If the multimedia content is digital, it can be included in the corresponding chapter as a hyperlink.

   ★ **Assessment:** After each class, student presenters administer the assessment tool.

After the assessments have been administered, the presenters can go over the answers with the class. Class discussion can focus both on what the presenters can teach their peers about writing as well as on what the assessment results can teach the presenters about how effectively they have achieved their learning goal.

 UDL Insight

When students consider how assessment results can help them understand the effectiveness with which they have met their learning goals, they are inquiring into a key tenet of UDL pedagogy. Whereas traditional educational theory assumes that the burden of understanding is on the learner, UDL emphasizes the role of the teacher in communicating information in ways that are accessible to the students. For UDL-oriented teachers, assessments evaluate the teacher's effectiveness, not the students' abilities.

8. Now that the handbook has been compiled and published, it can be used as a resource throughout the rest of the class. Consider using the handbook the way you would use a professionally published resource. Make the handbook available in a shared digital space (if possible, consider printing out hard copies for students to keep), use the handbook as a starting point for introducing lessons and assignments, and direct students to review certain chapters as needed.

ADDITIONAL SUGGESTIONS:

★ If you're repeating this assignment with future classes, consider using the previous class's handbook as a starting point for new content. New students can assess the strengths and weaknesses of the handbook compiled by their predecessors, filling in missing pieces, revising previous entries, or elaborating underdeveloped elements.

★ Steps 5–7 enhance the impact of the assignment by multiplying the means of engagement, representation, and expression, but skipping these steps might be appropriate for a classroom setting where the emphasis is entirely on producing alphabetic text.

★ The list of topics available to students can be adapted to the instructional needs of the class. An ESL class, for example, may be asked to select a topic that is more technical, while a first-year college composition class may focus more on elements of the writing process.

Writer's Vision Board

Writing is an extremely personal experience. Not only does the process of writing allow writers to express their language and their ideas, but students write in different ways, in different contexts, and for different reasons. The more students can reflect on their own writing habits and attitudes, the more self-aware they can become about how they work, and the more empowered they can be about how they manage writing projects. This activity is intended to encourage students to reflect on their writing experience from a range of perspectives and to share their insights with their classmates.

 UDL Overview

By the time students arrive in the classroom, they already have a lifetime of experience as writers. Some of this experience might be positive, some negative, but reflecting on this history early on in a writing class is an effective way to activate background information that students already have about writing, while also encouraging them to articulate the story of who they are as writers.

GOAL:

Encourage students to reflect on their own experiences as writers, activate students' background knowledge about the writing process, and expose students to strategies and perspectives that can empower them as writers.

YOU WILL NEED:

Access to Canva or a similar online whiteboard tool

TIME:

Three or four class sessions (with an extra component toward the end of the class)

OUTCOMES:

Students will:

- ★ identify multimedia items that express their habits and identity as writers

- ★ create a vision board that provides a visual representation of their identity as writers

- ★ compare different ways of writing, different writing strategies, and different ways of thinking about the aims of writing itself

- ★ learn about a variety of writing habits and strategies and consider integrating promising ideas into their own practice

- ★ appraise the evolution of their writing identity from the beginning of the class to the end

UDL Insight

This activity aligns particularly well with the UDL principle of providing options for self-regulation. In articulating a narrative about students' evolution as writers, the activity "promote[s] expectations and beliefs that optimize motivation" while also developing skills of "self-assessment and reflection."

DIRECTIONS:

1. Facilitate a class discussion where students reflect on the following questions. Students can choose which questions they want to answer, or the whole class could go through each question one at a time. This conversation could also be formatted as a think-pair-share or breakout group activity.

    ★ What is a positive experience that you have had as a writer?

    ★ What is a negative experience that you have had as a writer?

    ★ When you have a writing project, how do you go about managing your time?

    ★ When you write, where are you?

    ★ What kinds of conditions help you write at your best?

    ★ What do you like most about writing?

    ★ What do you like least about writing?

    ★ What role do you think writing has played in your life?

    ★ What role do you think writing will play in your future?

    ★ Why do you write?

Composition Connection

Writing effectively is just as much about mastering executive function skills as it is about sentence structure and content knowledge. The most important first step for any writing project is finding a place and time to sit down and do the work, a step that may be challenging for some students for a variety of reasons. Inviting students to reflect on this important aspect of their writing process allows them to identify challenges and consider possible solutions.

2. Following this class discussion, ask students to collect photos, artifacts, links, writing samples, or other material that reflects some aspect of how they work as writers and how they think about their identity as writers. Examples of such items may include:

   ★ a photo of their writing space

   ★ a copy of something they've written, whether for an academic purpose or a personal one

   ★ a photo of a journal or diary that they have kept at some point

   ★ photos of family members and friends who motivate them

   ★ images of favorite writers

   ★ inspirational memes, gifs, or quotations

   ★ a link to music that they listen to while they write

   ★ an image of a teacher who has inspired them (or has left them uninspired)

   ★ images of or from books they've loved

★ images representing subjects they have written about or hope to write about

★ images representing careers they hope to pursue through their writing

★ images representing their feelings (positive or negative) about the writing process

★ links to online content about writing that they have found helpful or motivational

★ A short personal quotation summing up their feelings about writing

★ anything else they can think of

Students should pick at least five such items to share with the class, then copy and paste their items into a Word document.

 AI Aside

In addition to generating text, AI programs can also generate images. An interesting way of experimenting with this technology is to ask an AI program to generate a unique image that contributes a meaningful element to the students' vision board. Challenge them to prompt the AI program to generate some unique image that brings together different components of the vision board (e.g., Maya Angelou dancing on a rainbow) or that illustrates their unique constellation of interests (e.g., Mona Lisa eating a taco—this student likes art and Mexican food). Generating these images and sharing them with the classroom community can stimulate creative thinking and also open up conversations about social and ethical questions surrounding image-generating technology.

Here is an example of an overview that can be used to introduce the vision board project:

WRITER'S VISION BOARD PROJECT OVERVIEW

A vision board is a personal collage that provides a visual representation of a creative project you are trying to think through or a personal goal that you want to achieve. You can go online to see examples of vision boards, as well as articles full of suggestions about how to put them together.

As we begin this writing class, it will be helpful for you to examine your identity as a writer. What do you like and dislike about writing? What parts of writing do you think that you're good at, and what parts of writing are you confused or anxious about? What kind of process do you use when you are doing a writing project? What positive and negative experiences have you had with writing in the past, and how do you imagine that you might use writing in your future life? There are a lot of questions to consider when you try to articulate your identity as a writer, and they are all interconnected with one another. A vision board can be a powerful tool for getting a handle on a complex topic like this.

This project will take us through a process of brainstorming, assembling, publishing, and reflecting on our writer's vision boards. The vision board you create for yourself will hopefully be a source of self-awareness and motivation over the course of the rest of the class.

3. If the class meets in person, provide students with an opportunity to talk about their items. If you can, print out their Word documents so that the students can cut them up to separate the items and then practice arranging them on the whiteboard with magnets or on an easel-sized sticky note with tape. Which items seem related to one another? How do they fit together spatially and conceptually? How can the items be arranged in a way that reflects their relationship to one another and tells the story of the student's identity as a writer?

Students may work on arranging their images in pairs, small groups, or as a whole class. Encourage them to use this workshop-style time to brainstorm additional elements that they might want to include on their vision boards and to determine how they want to arrange their content.

In particular, consider suggesting certain layout ideas, such as:

★ a concept-map-style web, with a picture of the student at the center and branches reflecting their responses to some of the questions from step 1

★ a past-present-future triptych that arranges the student's writing experiences in chronological order

★ a diptych identifying positive and negative experiences that the student has or has had with writing

Most importantly, however, the student should use the layout of their vision board to reflect their feelings about the items they are including.

 UDL Insight

Multimedia materials such as photographs, videos, and music can provide a way in for students (and more advanced writers) who may not know where to begin when faced with a blank page. Extratextual elements serve as a concrete jumping-off point for writing projects, activating visual and auditory styles of thinking that can support and enrich the language skills that student writers are developing.

4. Using Canva or some other online whiteboard program, students can upload their digital elements, arrange them either according to a template or from scratch, and design the colors, borders, and other elements in ways that establish the "mood" of their vision board.

5. After developing their vision boards, they can submit them to a discussion board on the class's LMS so that they can all see one another's work. Once they have done so, students should have an opportunity to present their vision boards to their classmates, either through a written reflection essay, a vlog-style video, or an oral presentation, depending on their preference. The discussion about the students' vision boards should consider:

   ★ common features that connect different students' vision boards

   ★ common obstacles that frustrate writers, and strategies that help them persevere

   ★ strategies for writing productively, including time management, optimal environmental conditions, and the cultivation of a growth mindset

   ★ experiences that help writers feel more confident

6. After discussing one another's vision boards, students can identify and reinforce useful insights by writing up a brief reflection essay assessing their impressions of their classmates' work. This reflection essay provides students with an opportunity to address questions such as:

   ★ What recurrent themes did you notice in the vision boards?

   ★ What new ideas about writing did you discover from your classmates' vision boards?

   ★ Aside from your own, which vision board was your favorite, and why?

7. The Writer's Vision Board activity is particularly useful as an introductory project for a writing class. Toward the end of the class,

students can return to these vision boards and reflect on whether their experience in the class has altered any of their attitudes, extended their personal narratives, or produced new elements that might be reflected in an updated version of these projects.

As an exit assignment for the class, invite the students to identify an element from the writing class—a sample of their writing; a piece of feedback from you or a classmate; a photo of you, a classmate, or the whole class—to add to their vision board. They may also consider revising, enhancing, or rearranging the vision board in any way that seems to reflect the evolution of their identity as writers. Presenting their revised vision boards to the class and discussing why they made the changes they made provides an opportunity for them to integrate their recent writing experience with their sense of who they are as writers. It also allows you a chance to summarize critical insights from the class and to evaluate your own impact as a writing teacher.

ADDITIONAL SUGGESTIONS:

★ The reliance of this activity on visual elements provides an opportunity for students to reflect on the importance of alt-text captions to ensure the accessibility of their vision boards. Students may also brainstorm strategies for nonvisual approaches to this reflection project—for example, an audio montage, a 3D installation-style project featuring physical objects, or an oral narrative.

★ Students (or you) may print out paper copies of the vision boards and circulate them in class. Students would be able to write notes and feedback on these printouts to highlight features of their classmates' work that they admire or are curious to learn more about. This activity might supplement the discussion about the students' vision boards that takes place in step 5.

★ Students can be encouraged to keep their vision boards nearby as they work on future writing projects for the class. They can hang a printout of the vision board at their desk, tape a copy to the inside of their notebook, or use their vision board as their computer's wallpaper. In this way, the vision board can serve as a continuing source of motivation throughout the class.

Writing Journal Blog

In order for students to gain confidence and self-awareness as writers, it is important not only that they write on a regular basis, but also that they develop a habit of reflecting on what they've written, what they want to write, and why they write. Keeping a writing journal is a classic strategy used by both students and professional writers for facilitating a routine of reflection. This activity encourages students to maintain their own writing journals while also creating a classroom community in which the reflective writing that students do in their writing journals becomes part of a shared culture of metacognitive introspection.

 UDL Overview

There are many educational benefits to maintaining a writing journal, such as helping foster student engagement, facilitating the integration of new ideas, providing a therapeutic outlet for students to think through challenges and anxieties, and encouraging students to use their writing as a tool for self-understanding. From a UDL perspective, the open-ended personal inquiry that students conduct in a writing journal supports the development of self-regulation, particularly students' proficiency in "self-assessment and reflection" (9.3), and executive function, particularly their "capacity for monitoring progress" (6.4).

GOAL:

Establish and maintain a routine of reflective journaling that provides a space for students to think through questions related to their writing.

YOU WILL NEED:

Access to a blogging feature through an LMS or an online platform

TIME:

To be maximally effective, the journal routine should be established early in the run of the class, assigned at weekly intervals, and sustained throughout the class's duration.

OUTCOMES:

Students will:

★ compose periodic reflections on their experiences with their writing assignments

★ identify challenges they face as writers and brainstorm solutions

★ compare their own experiences with the experiences of their classmates as they are expressed in their blogs

★ publish their reflective writing for a general audience

★ reflect on their intellectual journey over the course of the writing class

DIRECTIONS:

1. The Writing Journal Blog assignment differs from the other activities described in this book since it is not a single project but takes place in installments over the course of the semester. It is important to establish a routine of journaling early on in the class. Indeed, rather than being a supplement to the work of composing more

formal writing assignments, the writing journal can be thought of as the backbone of the class—a record of personal exploration and growth that the formal writing assignments are intended to promote and support. The journal will be able to play this role most effectively if it is introduced in the first week of the class.

A helpful way to introduce this assignment is to host a discussion about the value of writing not only as a form of communication but also as a way of generating ideas and reflecting on experience. Students might discuss their own experiences with keeping a journal, for either academic or personal reasons, and consider why journaling can be an effective tool for inquiry and self-understanding. Although the students will be writing their blog posts individually, the shared conversation about their blogs helps establish the class as a "blogging community" involved in a collective rhythm of self-reflection.

 Composition Connection

Writing is a very personal, intimate activity. Even when a student is writing about something very objective or abstract, they are still using their own words, their own syntax, and their own voice. While some student writers can be intimidated by this kind of self-exposure, embracing one's personal writing style not only helps students become more fluent, confident writers, but can also empower students to believe in their style of self-expression and to claim ownership of their voice. In its emphasis on introspection and its detachment from more formal writing assignments, the journal writing activity provides students with opportunities to both develop their personal voice and examine how their personal writing style lays a groundwork for writing in other genres.

2. Set up the blog sites. Specify a particular platform that all of the students will use. Many students will probably require explicit instruction in setting up an account and getting their blog started. According to your preferences, the blog site can be in a closed environment, accessible only to the other students in the class (i.e., through the LMS) or it can be open to the web, hosted by WordPress, Wix, or another such platform. Encouraging all of the students to use the same platform will make it easier for them to visit one another's blogs. As they set up their accounts, students should give their blog site a personalized title ("My Writing Journey," "Randy's Writing Reflections," etc.).

3. Once their blog sites are set up, students are ready to start posting content. The class as a whole can participate in brainstorming what their first posts should be about. The initial post should be a chance for the student blogger to introduce themselves, reflect on their past experiences with writing, and articulate their specific goals for developing their talents as writers. The prompt for the first blog post may ask students to reflect on such questions as:

★ What is your favorite thing about writing?

★ What is an example of something you've written in the past that you're proud of?

★ What aspects of writing cause you anxiety or frustration?

★ What strategies do you use to overcome obstacles when you're writing?

★ What kind of feedback have you gotten in the past about your writing—positive or negative—and how did you feel about this feedback?

★ If you were going to have a career as a writer, what would you write about?

★ Where do you get your best ideas?

- ★ What advice do you have for your fellow students about writing?
- ★ What is the best thing about your writing?
- ★ What do you think you can improve about your writing?
- ★ Where do you find inspiration in your life?

Of course, there is no need for students to address all of these questions in a single post, but any one of them might be a good starting point, and students can also return to these prompts in future installments of their blogs.

Be sure to specify whether you want students to compose their blog posts in the form of prose paragraphs or whether students should feel free to experiment with other formats. The main goal of the blog-based writing journal is to promote reflection, and this might be easier for some students to achieve if they have the option to post multimodal content such as audio or video clips, drawings, infographics, photo essays, or any other medium capable of expressing their thoughts and feelings about their writing.

 AI Aside

One of these blog posts might be an opportune time for students to reflect on their own perceptions of how chatbots can be used and abused. While students likely hear a lot of opinions from their instructors about the dos and don'ts of AI assistance, their own experience as learners and as users of technology provides them with unique insights into the ethical and educational questions swirling around these innovations. Allowing students to work out their own thoughts and feelings about the utility of chatbots validates their perspective and gives them a voice in this ongoing cultural conversation.

4. Make it a routine. Schedule a specific day each week when blog posts are due and devote some time in class to using insights that students articulate in their blogs as a starting point for discussion and reflection. It may help to encourage open-ended, nonjudgmental reflection if these posts are graded on a pass/fail basis, without giving overly intrusive editorial feedback.

   As the class starts working on writing projects together, you may choose to pose prompts that invite students to reflect on specific stages of their writing process. The blog can be a space where students brainstorm ideas, catalogue perspectives from their research, work through questions of how to structure a piece of writing, draft out paragraphs, suggest revision strategies, and evaluate the success of finalized writing projects. But students should also have the opportunity to use this space in whatever way makes the most sense to them. They can freewrite about random ideas, address obstacles they encounter in their writing process, complain about the assignment, or do anything else. It's their blog page, after all. The ongoing nature of this activity is the most important part—that it becomes a habitual routine for both the individual students and for the class community as a whole.

5. Throughout the duration of the class, students should be encouraged to visit each other's blog sites, post comments, and link to their classmates' posts in their own blogs. An engaging way to begin a class session can be to ask students to talk about what they've posted on this week's blog. If a student writes a blog post that they would rather not make public, they can always leave it unpublished and share it with you privately.

   Students can also post drafts and revised versions of their work to the blog site. If they want to, they can share the blog posts containing their final drafts on relevant social media sites.

> ### 👁 UDL Insight
>
> Maintaining a thoughtful writing journal may be one of the most impactful things that a student (or professional) writer can do to develop their writing skills. In its open-endedness, personalization, adaptability, and accessibility, a journal activity enhances the "relevance, value, and authenticity" (7.2) of writing instruction at any level.

6. When the class is wrapping up, the students' blog pages can be an ideal place for reflecting on their experiences in the class. As in step 3, students can work as a class to brainstorm prompts for a summative blog post, which might include questions such as:

   ★ What was your most successful piece of writing that you produced over the course of the class? What did you like about it?

   ★ What assignment gave you the most difficulty? Why, and what did you do to overcome this difficulty?

   ★ How did feedback from your instructor and your peers help you develop your writing?

   ★ How do you think you will apply your writing skills in future academic and professional contexts?

   ★ What aspects of your writing would you like to continue to work to improve?

   ★ Do you have any unanswered questions about your writing or about writing in general that you would like to ask the instructor and your classmates?

This summative blog post can be incorporated into the class as part of the final exam, and/or it can become the starting point for ongoing instructor–student conferences.

ADDITIONAL SUGGESTIONS:

★ Now that they have established their blogs, you can encourage your students to continue them beyond the end of the class. Students may continue using the blog as a writing journal to reflect on future writing assignments, or they can take it in a different direction.

★ Several activities in this book (including the Me-Time Log, My Human Thesis, AI-Informed Drafting, and "Wrap Around" Feedback and Guided Revision) involve reflective writing activities. If a blog routine has been established, these reflective writing tasks can take place in the students' blogs.

Inspiration and Brainstorming

Where do new ideas come from? This may be one of the strangest, most imponderable questions known to human beings, but it is also an essential starting point for any writing project. As teachers, we want students to articulate "original ideas," but this simple-sounding, clichéd advice glosses over how *people come up with original ideas, a question that has baffled artists and thinkers since the dawn of time. If we expect students to come up with original ideas but are unable to provide them with any practical strategies for doing so, we are setting them up for failure. Teaching students to write therefore requires all teachers to wrangle with the eternal mystery of where ideas come from, and to invite students to work through this same question for themselves.*

Like all great philosophical conundrums, the question of where new ideas come from is inherently unanswerable. On the other hand, through the lens of UDL and the infinite variability of human brains and human experiences, we can consider the possibility that any idea can be "new," since it takes shape in the unique brain of a unique person at a unique point in that person's life. Any given piece of information takes on an unprecedented configuration and becomes incorporated into a network of associational meanings as it becomes part of the neuro-architecture of any given human being. The fact that Abraham Lincoln was assassinated in 1865 is a piece of information that we share as a human race, but for everyone living on the planet, that raw fact interacts with an individualized constellation of related thoughts, feelings, and impressions. The variations in these associations might be very subtle from person to person, especially between people with similar cultural backgrounds, but they are inevitably there. This means that any idea that anyone has is inherently original, but it may take some introspection for someone to tease out how exactly the idea sits in their worldview, and dialogue with other people might be necessary to help someone understand what is original about their idea. At their best, brainstorming activities activate this kind of introspection and stimulate this kind of interpersonal dialogue. In doing so, they leverage the neurological, cultural, and linguistic variability among students, putting it to work as an engine of creativity and novelty. Brainstorming activities push students and teachers not only to ponder the question of where ideas come from, but also to experiment with active strategies for summoning them forth.

Most importantly, examining the ways in which all of our own ideas are already original opens up the question of who we are, what distinguishes us, what motivates us, and what we have to say that may never have been said before. The search for original ideas is an introspective journey into the currents that shape who we are as individuals, as members of communities, and as projects of self-becoming. Pinpointing these original ideas; bringing them out into language and consciousness; and elaborating, communicating, and supporting them are all part of a living process of becoming more aware of who we are and how we fit into the world. If this sounds very lofty, it's because this excavation of selfhood and identity sits at the center of why it is worth writing in the first place and, in particular, why it is worth doing for human beings as opposed to AI programs. If you're looking for a three-paragraph essay that explains cell division, you'll probably get a better result from a computer than from a human student, so why should the human student even bother? But if you want a student to think deeply about the process of cell division—to generate original ideas rooted in that person's own unique perspective about life, death, reproduction, legacy, inheritance, randomness, and evolution—then the computer is suddenly useless. There is a sense in which AI programs, for all their astonishing capabilities, are singularly incapable of generating original ideas. They are very good at writing something in the style of an artist or genre, but they are incapable of saying anything that hasn't been said before—usually thousands of times—in the archive of data that they mine to tell them how their sentences should sound. This makes the pursuit of new ideas—the kind of work done in the brainstorming process—a uniquely human quest, one that speaks to the heart of what it means to be human, amid and through all our diversity and complexity.

The most productive brainstorming strategies involve personal reflection, social exchange, and a heavy dose of randomness. They flirt with surrealism and irony. They can result in high comedy, shocking contrarianism, or unlikely juxtapositions. Just like the human brain itself, they make connections between apparently far-flung ideas, they improvise solutions on the fly, and they reach out from themselves to absorb new information and unfamiliar perspectives. At their best, brainstorming exercises are expansive, experimental, creative, and fun, and, in this sense, they celebrate the essence of what it means to be human.

Me-Time Log

Sometimes the things we really love are so close to us that we don't even recognize how important they are to us. Expressing oneself in any medium provides an opportunity to identify the people, ideas, and values that inspire us, as well as to explore, analyze, and deepen our relationship with them. This project invites students to take a reflective stance toward their daily routines, thoughts, social interactions, and leisure activities as a way of unpacking the themes that inform their personal identities. These themes can become the starting points for ideas and perspectives that are authentically rooted in students' own lifestyles and value structures.

UDL Overview

UDL emphasizes the importance of providing students with multiple opportunities for establishing and sustaining a sense of engagement with their learning, as well as for developing self-awareness regarding their degree of psychological involvement in their academic pursuits. While all students become more adept learners when they feel more engaged in their education, they may vary widely in terms of what kinds of topics engage them, as well as in terms of what kinds of strategies work to get them involved and keep them focused. A UDL-informed approach to designing writing assignments begins with this principle of learner variability, empowering students to find a way into a writing project that works for them.

GOAL:

Nurture students' insight into the passions that inspire and motivate them as learners and as human beings.

YOU WILL NEED:

★ multimedia tools for recording log entries

★ LMS for uploading and sharing multimedia log entries

TIME:

★ two weeks for recording journal entries

★ one class session for debriefing and analysis

OUTCOMES:

Students will:

★ maintain a log dedicated to reflecting on their daily activity

* cultivate self-awareness about their routines and priorities
* express themselves in a medium of their choice
* analyze the meaning of their daily activities
* articulate connections between their extracurricular activities and their educational goals
* generate research and writing ideas based on their personal values
* support their classmates' efforts to generate research and writing ideas based on their personal values

 Composition Connection

The best way to encourage students to develop a personal connection to a writing assignment is to give them the opportunity to determine what they write about. While, for academic purposes, course goals may prioritize the genre of the research paper, authentic and original research can be conducted around literally any element of human reality. If the goal of the class is to provide a setting where students are likely to discover a personal connection with the act of writing, then encouraging them to think about what they research in their spare time—whether it's basketball statistics, celebrity gossip, hip-hop dancing, or any other cultural phenomenon—improves the odds of this goal being met. Students may be surprised to learn that professional writers develop entire careers writing about these subjects. Moreover, the personal connections students have with their own hobbies and interests provides them with unique insight that can become the basis for fruitful academic inquiry.

DIRECTIONS:

1. Begin the activity by presenting students with a "flash" journal prompt. They can record their response to the prompt either in writing, through a drawing, or with a personal photograph that they supplement with an alt-text caption.

   This is the prompt:

   ME-TIME LOG

   Identify something you did in your spare time in the last week.

   Try to pick an activity that you did for yourself, for your own reasons, rather than something you did for school or for some other, "external" reason.

   It could be anything—a show or movie you watched, a concert you went to, a sports event you watched or participated in, a night out with friends, an online article you read or video you watched, a conversation you had, a walk you took, a volunteer experience you participated in, or anything else.

   After describing the activity, answer two or three of the following questions:

   ★ Why did you do it?

   ★ What was fun about it?

   ★ Why do you find this activity fun?

   ★ What does it say about you as a person that you like this thing?

   ★ How does your enjoyment of this thing connect to your memories of the past and your hopes for the future?

   Give students time in class to articulate their response or allow them to do the journal entry as a homework assignment.

2. Invite students to share their journal entries with the class. In addition to asking students to think about why they like the things they

like, this conversation can also be a useful opportunity to talk about journal writing as a form of reflection and self-expression. The conversation may address questions such as:

★ What advantages might there be in keeping a daily record of your thoughts and feelings?

★ What strategies can we think of to make journaling a part of our daily routine? When can you fit it into your day (in the morning, before you go to bed, while dinner is cooking, etc.)?

★ What medium do we feel most comfortable using to express our thoughts? Some people might prefer writing, some people might prefer recording their voice, and some people might prefer to talk to a webcam. Feel free to experiment with different styles to find what works for you.

The conversation should provide students with strategies for maintaining their own daily me-time logs over the next two weeks.

 AI Aside

Once the students have compiled a list of interests that they have derived from their me-time logs, AI tools can help them brainstorm interesting facts, critical questions, and ongoing controversies related to these topics.

3. For the next two weeks, have students maintain their daily me-time logs. They may not be able to log an entry every day of the two weeks, but suggest a minimum of, for example, 10 entries over 14 days. The entries do not have to be very elaborate, but each one should model the in-class "flash" prompt in identifying a me-time activity and discussing it in terms of the student's motivations for engaging in that activity.

The class may move on to other in-class activities during the time that the students are maintaining their logs, or the logs could become the basis for class discussions throughout this period. In either case, check in with the students as often as possible for updates on the progress and/or challenges they are experiencing with the log assignment. These conversations can be opportunities to troubleshoot solutions for students who are having a hard time with this assignment. If it seems that students need extra time and structure to support their journaling, consider allowing them to work on their logs in class.

4. After the two weeks have elapsed, students will compose and articulate an overview report that summarizes their observations about their me-time logs. In a face-to-face class, the best way to present this report may be through oral reports in front of the class, but students may avail themselves of other media at their discretion.

As they collect their thoughts for their summary report, it would be helpful if the students have a chance to talk informally about how they feel about their logs. In pairs, groups, or discussion board pods, students should compare their impressions of their logs, focusing on questions like:

★ What did you spend the most time doing?

★ What would you like to spend more time doing?

★ What themes or values stand out to you when you review your record of log entries?

★ Why do you think these themes and values are important to you?

★ How do they shape the way you see your academic pursuits, your professional goals, and your personal choices?

★ What would you like to learn more about these values?

★ What would you like other people to know about these themes and values?

★ How could you express these themes and values in ways that get people's attention, convey the truths that are important to you, and make them think?

After talking through their own impressions with their classmates, students prepare and compose a final report that summarizes what they took away from the process of keeping their me-time logs.

 UDL Insight

When students work on long-term projects like the Me-Time Log assignment, it is important to provide options for "sustaining effort and persistence." Making the logs the subject of class discussion is an excellent way of sustaining engagement by "fostering collaboration and community."

5. Students present their summary reports to the class. As they do so, the other students in the class have the responsibility of brainstorming answers to the following question: Based on what your classmate has reported about their me-time activities, what kinds of research, inquiry, and scholarship is this person uniquely qualified to pursue?

Ask each student to come up with three answers that differ from those of their classmates. (If this exchange is taking place on a discussion board, students can scroll through their classmates' comments before posting their own answers to ensure that they're contributing novel ideas.) These suggestions may be serious or funny, based on things the student said in their summary report or on other observations, practical or outlandish—the goal of this activity is simply to generate ideas of any kind in prolific variety. The aim is not only for presenters to be flooded with research ideas based on their own interests and passions, but also for the whole class to practice free-form, open-ended speculation. Ideally, every student who participates in this activity will come away with an expansive range of starting points for future research and writing projects, while also feeling empowered to build connections between their own lives and the world of ideas.

ADDITIONAL SUGGESTIONS:

★ Journal activities like the Me-Time Log and the Writing Journal Blog (see Part I) are excellent opportunities for students to cultivate a writing routine. If they can get into the habit of writing at the same time in the same place every day, or most days, they can establish a writing schedule that becomes part of their daily rhythm. This kind of consistency can help make writing less intimidating and more fully incorporated into their sense of self.

★ This activity can also be extended throughout the semester or combined with other journal-based activities to entrench a sustained ethos of reflective writing. Students can also be encouraged to continue their journals beyond the end of the class.

★ If students run out of steam or hit a wall documenting their me-time, encourage them to think of other ways of documenting their inner life, things they would like to do if they could, their dreams (sleeping and/or waking dreams), or time they spend with the important people in their lives (an "other-time log").

Random Fact Fantasia

Inspiration is all around us. While great ideas always come from within, sometimes our best ideas are triggered or suggested by chance encounters with random pieces of information. This activity challenges students to flex their imaginations to elaborate multiple implications and applications of random facts. It also examines strategies for making novel connections between random pairs of facts, and for incorporating specific pieces of information into larger rhetorical structures. Students also brainstorm possibilities for adding detail and complexity to emergent writing projects.

 UDL Overview

Like UDL itself, this assignment is all about celebrating variability, promoting it, and using it in creative and transformative ways. Conducted in the right spirit, this activity should encourage students to immerse themselves in the diversity of ideas and perspectives and to challenge themselves to diversify their own ideas in the process, multiplying ways of seeing and ways of thinking.

GOAL:

Practice strategies for diversifying perspectives, generating ideas, and elaborating compositional structures.

YOU WILL NEED:

Internet access

TIME:

Two or three class sessions

OUTCOMES:

Students will:

- ★ research and identify surprising facts
- ★ brainstorm possible applications and contexts for a random fact
- ★ practice creative ramification and free association

- ★ evaluate the viability of proposed research projects
- ★ develop a proposed idea into a rough outline
- ★ practice citing information from an online source
- ★ brainstorm strategies for extending and elaborating an outline

DIRECTIONS

1. Challenge students to go online and find three interesting, surprising, or thought-provoking facts. If they have an ongoing writing project, they can search for facts related to their research projects; otherwise, they can simply scan their social media feeds, surf through some of their favorite websites, or do a search for "interesting facts." Whenever possible, they should attempt to trace their interesting fact to an authoritative source.

   Once they have their three facts, they can write each one down on a separate piece of paper or, if it is an online class or if it seems more manageable to do it electronically, students can post their facts and links into a shared online document.

AI Aside

One way of finding interesting facts is to ask a chatbot to generate "three interesting facts." When I put this prompt into ChatGPT, it generated facts related to other prompts I had recently submitted, meaning that the facts were related to topics that I was supposedly interested in. If students want to use a chatbot-generated "fact" for this assignment, they should be sure to do the necessary detective work to confirm that it is true.

2. In pairs or individually, assign students three of the random facts from the list. Their job is to select one of the facts that they want to work with, and then come up with a list of different possible research projects that could conceivably incorporate this fact. They should consider questions such as:

   ★ How could this fact be part of a larger discussion?

   ★ What could this fact be used to demonstrate?

   ★ What are different ways that you could explain why this fact might be significant?

   ★ What is surprising about the fact, and how does it challenge our expectations?

   ★ What can we do with this random fact?

   ★ How does it or could it fit into wider conversations?

   Here is an example of a random fact, followed by a brainstormed list of possible contexts for the fact.

   Random fact: A crocodile cannot stick its tongue out.

   ★ comparison of tongues in different animals

   ★ crocodile anatomy and behavior

   ★ conservation status of crocodile species

   ★ adaptations that help crocodiles hunt

   ★ adaptations that help crocodilians hunt (alligators, caimans, etc.)

   ★ adaptations that help animals hunt

   ★ anatomy and physiology of the tongue across species

   ★ cultural significance of sticking one's tongue out

- ★ cultural significance of "biting one's tongue"
- ★ the spelling and etymology of the word "tongue"
- ★ medical concerns associated with biting one's tongue
- ★ representations of crocodiles in popular culture
- ★ fears associated with crocodiles, reptiles, carnivores
- ★ personal feelings/fears about crocodiles
- ★ does "Lyle, Lyle, Crocodile" stick his tongue out?

Brainstorming ideas can be more obvious and less obvious, more literal or more figurative, straightforward or slightly zany. As long as there is some connection to the original fact, the idea is valid.

Students should also be reassured that they don't need to have any expertise or prior knowledge about the topics they generate.

Challenge students to come up with as many possible answers as they can generate in 5 or 10 minutes, and consider making it competitive, with a prize for the individual or group who comes up with the most plausible contexts for their fact.

Students should record their ideas on an LMS discussion board or in a shared online document.

3. (Optional) If students are up for a bigger challenge, they can choose a second random fact from their pile and see if they can generate any research topics capable of encompassing both facts.

Random fact #2: Australia is wider than the moon.

- ★ survey of Australian crocodile species
- ★ ecological issues related to human/crocodile relations in Australia

★ lunar influences on crocodiles and other animals

★ Crocodile Dundee as an iconic representation of white Australian manhood

4. Following the activity, every team should have an opportunity to share their lists of ideas with their classmates, with a particular emphasis on identifying which of their ideas seems the most promising as the basis for an actual writing project. During the discussion, students can also talk about how they generated their ideas, and they can also help one another elaborate their lists with further suggestions from the group. Additional ideas arising during class discussion should also be added to the collective list.

5. Each student picks a topic from the list of writing project ideas suggested by the random facts. They can choose one of their own ideas or select another idea from the collective list. Encourage students to choose a topic that interests them, although, again, there is no need for them to have any prior knowledge about the topic.

As homework or as an in-class activity, students develop a rough outline based on the idea they are working with. It's important to emphasize that this outline is not a formal document or anything that they will be required to develop further; it can just be a list of things that the student would expect to see discussed in a piece of writing devoted to the topic they have chosen. Ideally, the outline will have at least three parts—a beginning, a middle, and an end—with some ideas about what the content of each section of the essay would cover. Students may submit the outline as a written document, or they can make their own notes and share them orally with the class.

>  **UDL Insight**
>
> Brainstorming is a crucial executive function, and one that often goes unaddressed in academic environments since it takes place (or is supposed to take place) "in the background" of more visible outcomes, such as an essay draft or project proposal. Like any skill, however, brainstorming needs to be explicitly demonstrated, discussed, and nurtured, since it is inevitable that some students will have less practice, facility, and confidence generating ideas than others. Teaching students to come up with new ideas, and to believe in their ideas, supports "planning and strategy development" (6.2), and discussing the applicability of random online facts facilitates students' fluency in "managing information and resources" (6.3).

6. Each student runs through their outline with the class. As they do so, the student's classmates brainstorm ideas for elaborating or expanding on the rough outline. As with the original brainstorming activity, students can work in pairs or individually, and the activity can be competitive or merely collaborative. Students should share their suggestions on an LMS discussion board, with a new post for each student outline.

   Whereas the first stage of this activity involves thinking "outwardly" into all the possible connections that radiate from the random facts, this stage of the activity brainstorms "inwardly" into the structure of a particular writing project. Students should consider what else they know about the topic that might be relevant to the discussion and what kinds of information they would expect to see in a piece of writing about this particular topic. As a class, they can also consider how these new perspectives might be added to the original outline to tell a coherent and comprehensive story. As the list of ideas connected to each outline grows, students perceive how the brainstorming process can develop rough outlines into more elaborate structures.

This activity is intended to be primarily a thought experiment and, as such, it works best if there is no expectation that any concrete writing assignment will be required as an outcome. For the purposes of the brainstorming exercise, there is no need for the writing projects to be developed any further than the rough outlines. That said, however, if any students do feel that their outlines are going somewhere and want to pursue them further, they should certainly be encouraged to do so, perhaps by using their outlines as the basis for a future writing assignment.

ADDITIONAL SUGGESTIONS:

★ This activity also provides an excellent opportunity to discuss the reliability of information found online, since many of the "facts" that turn up in the internet's many lists of interesting facts turn out to be partially or even completely nonfactual.

★ If students are stumped about how to develop their random-fact-based topic into an outline, they can ask a chatbot to do it and see what it comes up with. The chatbot's answer might give them some ideas that they can use as a starting point.

Multidisciplinary Wonderball

In this interactive game, students consider research topics from a variety of disciplinary connections. The activity is intended to open students up to new perspectives, incentivize them to ask and answer probing questions, and demonstrate the value of disciplinary and interdisciplinary ways of thinking.

UDL Overview

The variety of disciplinary perspectives considered in this activity provides multiple ways for students to engage with their research topics, and the randomized intersections of topics, disciplines, and students also stimulates engagement by facilitating a lively succession of shifting social and informational exchanges.

GOAL:

Recruit student involvement in the generation of new perspectives on specific research topics.

YOU WILL NEED:

A ball

TIME:

One or two class sessions

OUTCOMES:

Students will:

- ★ apply disciplinary perspectives to a variety of research topics
- ★ generate novel research questions
- ★ enhance their understanding of topics they are involved in researching
- ★ respond spontaneously and creatively to randomized intersections of topics and disciplinary perspectives
- ★ evaluate the viability of different research questions

- ★ consider the value of multi- and interdisciplinary perspectives as a tool for thinking and writing

- ★ use research questions to develop their understanding of a research topic

 Composition Connection

Explicit instruction in "writing across the disciplines" helps students make connections between the rhetorical tools they practice in the composition classroom and the more content-based curricula of their other classes. It also invites analysis of how different academic fields are characterized by a variety of ways of thinking, as well as by discipline-specific concepts, vocabularies, and rhetorical conventions. As students practice expressing ideas through the lens of different disciplines, they develop a sense of ownership and identification with these styles of discourse that can help them feel that they have a voice within a disciplinary conversation.

DIRECTIONS:

1. Introducing this activity provides an opportunity for a class to consider the various academic disciplines that make up the world of intellectual activity. Students can brainstorm a list of specific disciplines they are familiar with, a conversation that can address the wide diversity of fields of study and show how disciplines both overlap in various ways and branch off into subdisciplines. The class might consider visiting a university website to survey the different departments that the school comprises.

The result of this part of the activity should be a list of broadly applicable disciplines (as opposed to subdisciplines), which might look something like this:

Economics	Politics
Law	Art
Psychology	Physical Sciences
History	Business/Marketing
Social Justice	Media/Representation
Technology	Philosophy
Healthcare	Ecology/Sustainability
Religion/Spirituality	Sociology

Write the name of each discipline on a piece of paper. There should be one paper for each student. If there are more students in the class than there are disciplines on the list, duplicate some of the disciplines so that every student has a paper that identifies the disciplinary perspective they are responsible for considering.

2. Produce the "Wonderball" (which can be anything—a tennis ball or beach ball, or just a token classroom object like a stapler).

   One student volunteers or is chosen to share the topic of a research project they are investigating. The Wonderball represents the student's topic (e.g., black holes, Abraham Lincoln, access to mental health care).

   Sitting in a circle, the students (with the exception of the Wonderball student) pass the Wonderball around from left to right, all while singing or chanting (or listening to you sing or chant) a variation on the Wonderball song:

   The Wonderball goes round and round
   To catch it quickly you are bound

If you're the one to hold it last
A question you're required to ask!
You... are... it!

When the song is over, the student holding the Wonderball becomes the disciplinary expert on the Wonderball student's research topic. They must ask a research question that someone in their discipline might ask about the research topic.

For example, if the research topic is "access to mental health care," appropriate disciplinary questions might look like this:

History

★ How did people receive access to mental health care in the past?

Art

★ Can art therapy help to provide an accessible form of treatment?

Religion/Spirituality

★ What role can or do faith-based institutions play in helping people access mental health services?

The Wonderball student is responsible for recording all of the research questions into their notes.

This activity is pretty fast-paced, so it should be possible, depending on the temperament and size of the class, to do 5 to 10 rounds for each Wonderball student.

After the Wonderball student has recorded research questions from 5 to 10 fellow students, it becomes another student's chance to be the Wonderball student.

Everyone else in the class rotates or shuffles their disciplines for the next research topic, and the game resumes.

Depending on the class dynamic, you can determine whether the game itself is the best time to follow up on examining possible answers to the students' research questions. As interesting as these questions might be, it may be better for the class to stay focused on generating questions in this part of the activity and to save the answering for the next step.

 AI Aside

As part of the process of answering the questions generated by the Multidisciplinary Wonderball activity, students can type their questions into a chatbot and see what the chatbot has to say. Since this activity is not a writing assignment, plagiarism is not really an issue. The students should feel welcome to consult the chatbot response in the same way they would consult an online article or a comment from a classmate: as another perspective to consider as they formulate their own stance.

3. After the Wonderball game, each student should have a list of interdisciplinary questions about their research topic. Students should each pick three of the questions that they find the most thought-provoking, for whatever reason, and respond to them. Since the Multidisciplinary Wonderball activity is primarily a thinking exercise rather than a writing project, the students don't have to respond to the questions in writing, although they are welcome to do so if that option appeals to them. Alternatively, they can express their reflections on the questions through a vlog, podcast, or oral report.

For each student-generated research question, the student researcher should address the following prompts:

★ Answer the question (to the best of your ability, or propose possible answers).

- ★ What facts or data support your answer(s) to the question?
- ★ Why do you feel that this question is particularly interesting or important?

Students should make their responses available to their classmates through the class's LMS.

 UDL Insight

As with most brainstorming activities, the goal of Multidisciplinary Wonderball is not necessarily to learn new things but to spark connections among pieces of information that the student already has access to. The activity combines spontaneous and reflective modes of thinking, as well as a social component and a solitary component, as a way of providing multiple means for activating background knowledge (3.1), highlighting patterns and relationships (3.2), and maximizing transfer and generalization (3.4).

4. Facilitate a class discussion in which each student talks about one of the three questions they chose to write about. The primary goal of this discussion should be to illustrate how a compelling research question can develop into a writing project:

- ★ How can the answer to the question be phrased as a thesis statement?
- ★ What information would students need to learn in order to develop their answers in greater detail?
- ★ How might a long-form composition about this research question be structured?

But it can also be illuminating to use this opportunity to think about the logic of the activity itself:

- ★ What is the value of disciplinary perspectives?

- ★ Are there disadvantages or limitations that go along with disciplinary thinking? In addition to serving as a lens, can they also serve as blinders or vectors of tunnel vision?

- ★ Which disciplines do individual students tend to gravitate toward, and which disciplines seem more opaque or unwelcoming? Why?

- ★ How can multiple disciplinary perspectives supplement one another to create a richer understanding of a research topic?

Ideally, students will come away from this activity with both a wide variety of perspectives on their research topics as well as a deeper comprehension of the relationships among different fields of knowledge.

ADDITIONAL SUGGESTIONS:

- ★ In a synchronous online class, with live discussion, instead of having the students circulate the physical Wonderball, you can ask them to find a physical object in their remote environment to use as their personal Wonderball. As you read off their names in alphabetical order, they sing the Wonderball song and hold up their Wonderballs in front of the screen when it is their turn. The student holding up their Wonderball at the end of the song is "it." The list of disciplines can be posted in the comment section, assigned before the first round, and then rotated for each new round.

- ★ In an asynchronous online class, this activity can take place on a discussion board. First, each student posts their research topic, and all students are randomly assigned a list of (for example) five disciplines. Then, students have to post five response comments to five different research topics, articulating questions suggested by each of their assigned disciplines.

- ★ In a discipline-focused composition class, this assignment can be tweaked to cover subdisciplines. In a biology class, for example, the list of subdisciplinary perspectives might include genetics, ecology, evolutionary science, anatomy, physiology, biochemistry, cytology, sociobiology, and paleontology. A literary studies class can use the same activity to examine texts from various critical perspectives: psychoanalytical, deconstructionist, social justice studies, ecocritical, and the like.

Research

Research is a collective, all-encompassing word. It refers both to the act of seeing information as well as to the sources of information themselves. There is a tendency to talk about a "research process" as if there were a specific formula to follow for gathering information; there is also a tendency to think of the research process as distinct from the "writing process," as if they were two different things. All of these impressions belie the complexity and interactivity involved in any meaningful research experience, which can be a transformative journey of discovery.

If students are inquiring into a topic that is meaningful to them, they probably already have a "personal database" of information, opinions, assumptions, and value judgments that provide a necessary starting point. In a sense, the students themselves are the first experts they should consult, and offering students a variety of opportunities for thinking through these attitudes can help them not only articulate what they already know but also become more aware of their own attitudes. The first step of the research process doesn't necessarily involve logging on to the internet, but rather tapping into the unique structures of prior knowledge that the students already possess. In a classroom environment, this background knowledge not only is personal to individual students but also can be activated as a collective resource, where students' various backgrounds and experiences can help provide contexts and contrasts for one another's perspectives. Classroom discussions that invite students to talk about research topics from their different points of view can generate baseline insights that future research may reinforce, contest, or modify.

Research can take many forms beyond the classroom as well. Since information comes in so many different forms, the project of conducting research can be an opportunity for students to think reflectively about what sources of information seem particularly relevant and productive for them. While some students may find that reading scholarly articles about a topic can reveal useful perspectives, academic forms of knowledge are most likely to be relevant if they are supplemented with other forms. In addition to engaging in personal introspection and discussion with their peers, both of which qualify as forms of research, researchers conduct observations; confer with experts; consult documentaries, blogs, and journalism; participate in social media exchanges; reflect on fiction and art; and maybe even plug prompts into an AI chatbot. Immersing themselves in these various streams of discourse, researchers expose themselves to the diverse possibilities latent within their research topics, and they also build fluency in the multivalent languages of the information ecology, which is itself continually diversifying and evolving. Indeed, developing an adaptive and responsive relationship with sources of information may ultimately be a more valuable outcome for student researchers than the "content" of what they are learning about. The more fervently we encourage students to explore the possibilities, pathways, and (potentially) perils of this information ecosystem, the more prepared they will be to feel empowered, rather than overwhelmed, by its diversity.

The research activities included in this handbook encourage students to consult a wide variety of sources, and they can certainly be used in combination to enrich the depth and texture of students' research process. Inspired by UDL principles, these activities embrace the different media, channels, and forms of discourse—the many "multiple means" of learning new things—and also invite students to play an active role in responding to research sources, taking ownership of them, and drawing them into conversation with a wider community of fellow students and other researchers. This combination of a variety of sources and myriad opportunities for interacting with them allows students to work with new information in meaningful and original ways. In the process, students transform themselves from learners into experts, using the same techniques of immersion, reflection, and conversation that professional experts use to acquire fluency in their disciplinary fields.

Show-and-Tell Multimedia Bibliography

Even for students who feel passionate about their research project, research itself can sometimes feel like a grueling and lonely slog. This activity reinvents the traditional "annotated bibliography" assignment, opening it out both to a more robust multimedia definition of what qualifies as a research source and to a more interactive discussion with the classroom community about how researchers work, the value of different kinds of sources, and the applicability of specific sources to students' own research questions.

 UDL Overview

This activity highlights the many different ways that researchers gather information. While a conventional annotated bibliography privileges the written word as both the most valued source of information and as the expected means of evaluating and commenting on sources, this activity encourages students to think broadly about the various ways that people learn about the world around them, and it leverages the social dynamic of the classroom as an opportunity for students to reflect on what they're learning about in their research process. In doing so, the show-and-tell-style bibliography employs multiple means of representing and processing new information.

GOAL:

Support students as they explore a diverse range of research sources and consider the applicability of different sources to a central research question.

YOU WILL NEED:

★ access to databases of multimedia research materials
★ a website or LMS for hosting students' research notes

TIME:

Four or five class sessions

OUTCOMES:

Students will:

★ familiarize themselves with a variety of means for gathering information about a research topic
★ brainstorm research strategies
★ conduct research around a specific research question
★ evaluate the applicability of specific research sources to a given research project
★ summarize information found in research sources
★ identify quotes and facts from their research that can help them respond to a research question
★ compare the advantages and limitations of different kinds of research sources
★ develop a strategy for incorporating information from their research into an emergent research project
★ discuss and reflect on their research experience

DIRECTIONS:

1. Begin by hosting an informal discussion about where students get information from in their own lives. A good way to start this

conversation is by asking the students to think about the last time they learned something new. Where did they learn it from? It is likely that the students will respond with a variety of answers, including social media content, teachers, conversations with other people, news programs, online ads, and maybe even print sources. Keep a running tally of these different kinds of information sources, emphasizing their variety and also considering their comparative merits and disadvantages regarding critical characteristics such as reliability, accessibility, and level of informational detail.

The outcome of this discussion will be a list that looks something like this:

Professional research journals	Popular/general audience magazines
Articles from online or print-based newspapers	Journalistic podcasts or television series
Websites/social media pages	Nonfiction books
Documentaries/online videos	Works of fiction
AI chatbots	Human beings (interview subjects/experts/teachers)
Other	

 AI Aside

The brainstorming discussion in the first step of this activity is an opportune time to discuss the value of AI programs as research tools. Used appropriately, these programs can help writers locate information and even suggest strategies for making arguments and structuring a piece of writing. It is also important, however, to discuss the biases and limitations inherent in these tools.

2. Once the list of different kinds of sources has been compiled, students can conduct a scavenger hunt–style research process centered on their (preselected) research topics. Depending on the focus of the class, students might be challenged to find one source of information about their topic from three different kinds of sources, or they can be encouraged to use whatever sources seem most likely to provide them with the kind of information they will need to write intelligently about their topics. Either way, this process invites students to consider the advantages and disadvantages of different kinds of sources, specifically as they relate to their own research projects.

 UDL Insight

Encouraging students to explore a range of research sources provides them with multiple options for gathering information. For students who, for whatever reason, have trouble decoding textual research sources, conducting surveys and interviews provides another way in to the research process. Meanwhile, students who typically rely on textual research sources can expand their research toolkit by experimenting with these interpersonal techniques.

3. Students prepare a four-slide PowerPoint presentation. The first slide should present the research question they are investigating, and the next three slides should each highlight one of the sources that the student found about their topic. In the slideshow, students can share a link to each source (or whatever other identifying information might apply). If it is easier, they can bring a hard copy of the source (a printout of an article they read, a DVD they watched, a copy of a book

they read, etc.) to class. The students should prepare answers to the following questions:

★ What is the main point expressed in the source?

★ What is the most interesting piece of information you found in this source?

★ Identify an interesting pull quote from the source.

Depending on what works better for the class, students may write out answers to these questions in their PowerPoint slides, prepare notes for themselves to share with the class, or simply answer the questions in their heads.

4. Students prepare their show-and-tell presentations. Either in live presentations or through prerecorded video presentations, students "show" their research source (whether digital, physical, or other) and "tell" their classmates about how the information from each source advances their research project.

As they watch their classmates' presentations, students respond in writing with feedback to the presenters, addressing the following questions:

★ What was the most interesting aspect of the researcher's presentation?

★ What additional questions do you have about the researcher's topic?

★ What other sources do you think the researcher might consider consulting?

Students can post their responses to these question to a shared discussion board, giving each researcher multiple suggestions for moving forward with their research project. Students' responses to one another's presentations also provide robust opportunities for class discussion and instructor input about such topics as:

★ the strengths and weaknesses of specific kinds of sources

- ★ the scope, focus, and framing of students' research projects
- ★ additional resources that students may not be aware of
- ★ opportunities for students who may be researching similar topics to share research sources with one another
- ★ the possibility of students pooling each other's own expertise and perspective as a research source

5. A brief, low-stakes reflection assignment is a useful way to provide some closure to this activity. After presenting their research and receiving their classmates' feedback, students can respond in writing or in some other format to the following prompt:

How has your research process shaped your thoughts and feelings about your research topic? What feedback from your classmates did you find helpful, and where do you want to go next with your research project?

ADDITIONAL SUGGESTIONS:

- ★ In asynchronous online classes, students can record their show-and-tell presentations and post the video or audio files to a discussion board, allowing their classmates to respond with their answers to the discussion questions in step 4.

- ★ Examining the sources that students bring in to discuss can be a good opportunity to look for information about whether the source accepts submissions, letters, or other opportunities to "talk back." If the source is an academic journal, a blog, a newspaper, a social media page, or some other format that provides opportunities to respond to the content, you can encourage students to develop their research project as a potential publication through that source.

Community Survey and Personal Interview

Communicating with other people is one of the most productive activities that any researcher in any field can engage in. Not only can other people introduce researchers to valuable information and perspectives, but the experience of talking about what they are researching requires a researcher to think more deeply about their own work and their own ideas. This activity invites students to think about what they can learn about their topic from the other people in their immediate environment, deepening their personal engagement with their research topics while also providing practice in quantitative and qualitative aspects of research methodology.

 UDL Overview

For many people, social interaction is uniquely motivating and meaningful. While academic research is typically thought of as an isolating and even antisocial pursuit, the social dimension inherent in all human knowledge means that there is always something to learn from talking to people and listening to their points of view. Conducting surveys and personal interviews exposes students to socially interactive forms of research, but it also allows them an array of both quantitative and qualitative ways of interpreting the results of their inquiry.

GOAL:

Foster students' ability to assess personal attitudes, pervasive opinions, and social contexts that are related to their research topics.

YOU WILL NEED:

Paper and printer for printing out surveys/questionnaires (for face-to-face classes)

TIME:

Two to three weeks

OUTCOMES:

Students will:

★ learn techniques for developing surveys, questionnaires, and interview questions

★ design and conduct surveys, questionnaires, and interviews

★ practice interpersonal skills in their role as researcher

★ interpret quantitative and qualitative data

★ consider research topics from social and interpersonal perspectives

★ evaluate the relevance of different forms of data for a given research project

★ synthesize research findings to articulate a summative assessment

DIRECTIONS:

1. A great way to begin this activity is by designing a brief multiple-choice survey for the students to take at the beginning of a class session. The survey might ask them about their feelings about the class so far, their evolving thoughts about their research projects, or even what they know and how they feel about taking surveys. Conducting this survey through an online tool will allow the results to be recorded and charted out instantaneously.

   Ask students to respond to the survey results. Did the results surprise them or match their expectations? Did any of the questions stand out as ambiguous or confusing? What other questions might be added to the survey? How did they feel as "subjects" taking the survey? How do they feel about taking surveys in general? What role do surveys, questionnaires, and personal interviews play in scientific, academic, and professional inquiry?

In particular, this conversation should lead students to think about what they can learn about their research topics by employing these data collection tools. Each student should write out a research question related to their topic that they can investigate by canvassing other people's attitudes and opinions.

 UDL Insight

Encouraging students to explore a range of research sources provides them with multiple options for gathering information. For students who, for whatever reason, have trouble decoding textual research sources, conducting surveys and interviews provides another way in to the research process. Meanwhile, students who typically rely on textual research sources can expand their research toolkit by experimenting with these interpersonal techniques.

2. Now each student creates a survey designed to collect data related to their research question. They should each articulate at least five questions for the survey. As they work on composing these questions, the class can discuss critical questions related to survey design, including:

   ★ comparative advantages and disadvantages of online versus pen-and-paper surveys

   ★ comparative advantages and disadvantages of open-ended versus closed-ended questions

- ★ an overview of online survey tools
- ★ discussion of the ethics of survey design and analysis:
  - ★ leading questions
  - ★ sample size, random sampling, and generalizability
  - ★ informed consent of survey subjects
  - ★ "cherry-picking" data
  - ★ confidentiality

Invite students to discuss their survey questions with one another and to provide feedback and suggestions to their classmates.

3. Have students conduct the surveys. They can complete surveys for one another or conduct the survey outside of class.

    It is important to emphasize that this survey is for educational purposes only, and that no respondents should be pressured to respond to any survey question that they don't want to answer.

4. Students will design an infographic that displays their survey results. They can use the graphing function in Excel or a design tool like Canva to illustrate their findings.

 AI Aside

Students can use chatbots to help them brainstorm and articulate survey and interview questions. This process, however, should involve reviewing the chatbot's suggestions carefully to vet them for relevance and appropriateness.

5. Discuss the survey process with students, soliciting general impressions about what they expected, what they were surprised by, and

what other questions they have about their data. What questions would they like to dig more deeply into?

In order to pursue these questions, encourage students to identify someone that they would feel comfortable interviewing. You can partner students up into interviewing pairs, or students can choose to interview family members, other teachers, or friends outside of class.

At this point, the class can also discuss the kinds of questions that students might want to ask their interview subjects. As with the discussion about the surveys, this conversation should address the ethics and best practices associated with conducting person interviews, including:

- ★ the difference between survey questions and interview questions
- ★ the importance of informed consent and confidentiality
- ★ respect for the dignity and autonomy of the interview subject
- ★ the role of nonverbal behavior
- ★ techniques for recording and interpreting data from personal interviews

6. Have students conduct their personal interviews. These interviews should be brief and casual.

   As with the survey, it is important to remind students that interview respondents *should not feel pressured* to answer any questions they don't want to answer, and that *conditions of confidentiality do not apply* to this nonscientific, educational activity.

7. Students prepare a research report conveying their findings to the class. The research report may take the form of a PowerPoint presentation, but they may choose to share their findings in a different format if they prefer. The report should include the following elements:

   - ★ a statement of the student's original research question

- ★ a review of the survey results, featuring the infographic from step 4
- ★ a description of the personal interview, featuring:
  - ★ interview questions
  - ★ summary of attitudes and opinions expressed by the interview subject
  - ★ significant quotation(s) from the interview subject
- ★ conclusions
  - ★ How does data from the survey compare with the perspective articulated by the interview subject?
  - ★ What have you learned about your research topic from the people you have surveyed and interviewed?
  - ★ What new questions do you have about your research topic?

 Composition Connection

Composition instructors typically outsource the teaching of numeracy, or quantitative literacy, to their colleagues in math and statistics, but working thoughtfully with numbers is a critical part of academic writing. Students often use statistical data in research compositions, and this activity provides an opportunity for students to think through the ways that statistical information is collected and interpreted.

8. Provide students with an opportunity to respond to one another's research reports, either through a discussion board thread or in face-to-face/synchronous discussions. Encourage students to talk to one another about how their research findings might be developed into

further lines of inquiry, online articles for a general audience, or an academic journal article.

ADDITIONAL SUGGESTIONS:

★ While many students are engaged and motivated by opportunities for social interaction, other students might feel anxious or overwhelmed. It is important to provide these students with alternative means of conducting the survey (such as through an online survey tool) and the personal interview (for example, via email).

★ Of course, it is possible to modify this activity so that students do the survey but not the personal interview, or vice versa. Doing both affords the advantage of being able to compare and contrast different ways of collecting data, but either part of this activity can advance the overall goal of enabling students to canvass different perspectives about their research topics.

Email an Expert

Researching a topic in any field is a way of becoming part of a community of people who are curious about the same topic. Becoming conversant in a field of inquiry is like learning a language, and, as with learning any language, one of the best ways to do it is to communicate with people who speak the language fluently. This activity invites students to initiate conversations with members of the research community.

 UDL Overview

A key priority in UDL is developing students' perception of themselves as expert learners. Learning about and reaching out to an expert can empower students to participate in the conversations about their research topics and also to feel that, in doing so, they

> are laying claim to their own style of expertise. It may be useful to consider that being a so-called expert in a topic does not necessarily mean mastering a large number of facts; "expertise" can also mean having the ability to think about a topic in a new way or from a unique perspective, and being committed to thinking through the implications of that perspective. Expertise is also largely a social-consensual phenomenon. Experts are those who are in the social circle that is defined as having expertise. This activity spurs students to jump into this circle, thereby magically redefining themselves from learners into experts.

GOAL:

Empower students to "talk back" to experts in their research field in a way that encourages them to think both about what they can learn from the expert and about what the expert can learn from them.

YOU WILL NEED:

Access to email

TIME:

Two weeks

OUTCOMES:

Students will:

- ★ identify experts in their research field and learn about their careers
- ★ survey the scope of professional and academic work that constitutes the discourse of a given research field
- ★ practice professional etiquette in the composition of email correspondence

★ articulate research questions in response to the work of a particular expert

★ reflect on their own status as emergent experts and critique the concept of expertise as a social category

★ if possible, pursue correspondence with their expert

DIRECTIONS:

1. Scholars engaging in research are not only gathering information but also meeting a variety of people—the writers, academics, journalists, filmmakers, enthusiasts, and researchers who publish books, articles, chapters, blogs, and documentaries about their research topics. As they conduct their research, encourage students to identify a particular individual whose work they have consulted as part of their research activity.

   For the purposes of this assignment, it may be helpful to avoid focusing on "big names" in their field. For every big name or celebrity figure in a given field, there are typically hundreds of people working in relative obscurity, and it is likely that students will have more success soliciting a response from someone with a lower profile. Encourage students to think of a research source that has stood out to them for some reason or that has some particular relevance to their own research question and to consider selecting the author of that source as their expert for this project.

 AI Aside

One way of gathering information about an expert is to ask a chatbot program to compose a 500-word essay about that expert's work. Watch out, though! Checking the chatbot's response against independently verifiable information will likely demonstrate both the chatbot's impressive abilities as well as its limitations and proneness to error.

2. Next, students will learn as much as they can about their expert. They should develop a brief PowerPoint presentation containing key pieces of information about their expert, including:

   ★ the expert's email address (this is important—if the expert's email address is unavailable, the student will have to pick a different expert for this project)

   ★ the research source that introduced them to the work of this expert

   ★ where the expert works

   ★ what else the expert has published (in the field that the student is researching or in other fields)

   ★ the expert's presence on social media, if any

   ★ a photo of the expert

   ★ questions they have for the expert

Students should have an opportunity to share their profile of the expert with their classmates, with a particular emphasis on questions they would like to ask the expert. Discussion can touch on the different capacities in which experts work (in academia, in journalism, in the private sector, as online commentators, etc.). Students may also suggest additional questions that students might ask their experts.

 Composition Connection

Although it is rarely taught explicitly, composing emails is one of the most important kinds of writing that professional and academic personnel perform on a regular basis. Encouraging students to think about email as a genre of writing with its own stylistic conventions and decorum allows them opportunities for learning about how to express themselves creatively and effectively in this medium. This email activity also provides an object lesson in the importance that the written word continues to have in contemporary communication.

3. The students are now ready to compose email letters to their experts. This is an opportunity for students to discuss formality and courtesy in professional correspondence. Students may begin by brainstorming what they have learned previously about email etiquette, both to collectively develop a list of best practices and to apply these principles in their own letter.

   Students may also collectively discuss how they want to structure their letters, but each letter should include the following elements:

   a. Say what you liked about what the expert said.
   b. Demonstrate some knowledge about the expert's career.
   c. Explain your own research project.
   d. Ask a specific question about your research topic.
   e. Also ask: What else should I read?

4. After students compose their emails, the class should have an opportunity to read at least some of their classmates' letters. Doing so will give students a chance to proofread and fine-tune their messages, and it will also provide a chance for evaluating the letters' consistency with the email best practices covered in step 2.

   At the very least, each letter should undergo some kind of editorial review process with an eye toward optimizing both technical proficiency and collegial tone.

5. Have students send their emails and work on something else for a week.

6. A week after the emails are sent, reconvene to share results. It is likely that some students will have received responses from their experts, while others haven't.

   For students who have heard back from their experts:

   ★ How would you evaluate the quality of your expert's response?

   ★ What observations do you have about the style of the expert's response email? Does your expert obey email etiquette best practices?

- ★ What was helpful or not so helpful about your expert's response?

- ★ Will you write back to your expert, and, if so, what will you say?

Students who have not heard back from their experts can help assess the emails from the experts who have responded, but they can also address the question:

If you had to imagine what your expert would have written in their response, what would it say? (Be your own expert.)

Both groups can reflect on what they can learn about a research field by focusing not only on the content contained in research sources, but also on the people involved in creating that content.

ADDITIONAL SUGGESTIONS:

- ★ If it seems appropriate to do so, and if the means are available, students might consider contacting their expert through a social media platform instead of via email. This may result in a more immediate response, but this variation on this activity should also include a mini-lesson on the rules of professional etiquette associated with social media communication.

- ★ Students who hear back from their experts should be encouraged to sustain the correspondence, first of all by thanking the expert for writing back, and also in the interest of furthering their research project. In addition to asking follow-up questions about their research project, challenge them to find a quotation from the email exchange that they can incorporate into the text of their research project.

- ★ Keep the conversation open, since it is likely that students who don't hear back from their experts within the first week may receive responses eventually. Invite students to continue reporting to the class about their interactions with their experts.

Outlining

Any research-based writing project begins as a swarm of information and ideas. The brain is structured like an elaborate web, with every point connected to thousands of other points, all radiating outward and interconnected in dazzlingly complex ways. It is not surprising, then, that ideas tend to appear to consciousness as clusters of associations, more or less densely packed but generally sprawling, amorphous, and open-ended. Academic communication, however, has a very different geometry. Composing *in any genre means to arrange information into a structure. Writing is always one thing at a time, and one thing after another, in a linear progression from the first word to the last.*

One of the major challenges for most writers is translating the cloudy impressionism of thinking into rows of individual words and sentences. In traditional writing classes, the ubiquitous tool for organizing a piece of writing is the hierarchical outline, a list of talking points divided into subordinate categories and arranged in a sequence that mirrors their position in the essay that is being planned. Some students find this outline format familiar and intuitive, and helping students use some kind of outlining process to sort out their impressions of a topic is certainly an invaluable component of any writing curriculum. For other students, however, the conventional outline format can become a stumbling block rather than a stepping-stone. The rigid stylization of a standard alphanumeric outline can overwhelm some students, and even a bare outline doesn't make sense to every writer. Whereas the final composition is a necessary endpoint of an academic writing class, the outline is a means to an end, and so, in the interests of allowing writing students to take ownership of their planning process, it is worthwhile to imagine alternative strategies that students might use to organize the compositional structure of an essay they intend to write.

Cultivating a diverse toolkit of organizational strategies not only helps different writers find the approach that works for them, but also presents a diverse menu of choices that any one student may use for different kinds of projects with different topics and in different compositional genres. An organizational strategy that works for a research presentation might not work as well for a personal narrative essay, so practicing different ways of thinking through the structure of something they are trying to express enables students to become more flexible writers and thinkers. Different organizational strategies can also complement one another in ways that enhance writers' understanding of what they are trying to say. This means that a UDL-style buffet of outlining activities is helpful at the level of the classroom community, at the level of the individual student, and even at the level of an individual student's response to an individual writing project.

Any approach to organizing a composition presents an opportunity to think through the big questions of what you want to say, who you want to say it to, and why either of you should care. The activities in this section use both introspective and interpersonal techniques to provoke students into thinking through these big questions. They are designed to serve as a kind of scaffold for student writers as they work through the challenging process of developing nebulous impressions into formal rhetorical structures. As all writers know, the blank page can be a daunting challenge to face, but creative and adaptive outlining strategies can help populate that blank space with landmarks, anchor points, and pathways. Every student has ideas worth expressing, and a robust and creative outline can serve as a kind of instruction manual guiding them through the challenges of expressing these ideas with confidence and precision.

My Human Thesis

Conversations about articulating an appropriate thesis typically address technical questions like whether a given thesis is too narrow or too broad, whether it is too factual or too tendentious, and whether it is clearly or cloudily articulated. In the age of AI, however, it is important to ask a more profound question: How "human" is your thesis? This activity challenges students to identify a thesis for a research paper by thinking about their research through the lens of their own perspective and (human) experience.

 UDL Overview

Every student is different. Every writer is different. Every human being is different. In fact, writing can be thought of as a tool for showcasing a human writer's capacity to say things that have never been said before, and that could never be said in quite the same way by anybody else in the past, present, or future. The My Human Thesis activity begins by asking students to reflect on what it means to be human, and then welcomes them to use an array of expressive tools to explore their own uniqueness. While this activity is focused on a shared (and pretty pedestrian) outcome—the development of a thesis statement—it celebrates the infinite variety of questions that human beings can ask and the infinite ways in which that inquiry can be conducted.

GOAL:

Develop thesis statements for composition projects that are rooted in the personal associations and values that connect students to the topics they are writing about.

TIME:

Two or three class sessions

OUTCOMES:

Students will:

★ compare the expressive capabilities of human brains and digital text-generation programs

★ identify aspects of lived experience that are exclusive to human beings

★ investigate research topics through the lens of their unique human experience

★ conduct introspective analysis into their personal relationship with a research topic

★ discuss their introspective insights with classmates

★ use the results of their introspective analysis to formulate thesis statements for developing composition projects

DIRECTIONS:

1. This activity should begin with an open-ended discussion about the similarities and differences between human brains and AI programs. AI programs are capable of doing some of the same work that human brains do. For example, they can arrange information from different sources into sentences, paragraphs, and generic structures. At the same time, of course, there are basic elements of human reality that are beyond the understanding of any computer program, and these elements tend to be the foundation for most of what is meaningful in life and in writing. As a class, brainstorm a list of these elements and talk about what makes them uniquely human.

Different classes may identify different human elements, but seven that seem particularly salient to me include:

★ my sense of self

★ my social and family relationships

★ my memories of my past

★ my hopes for my future

★ my sense of justice and my moral values

★ my cultivation of physical and psychological wellness

★ my unconscious processes

Use class discussion to compile a list of human elements and use this list as the basis for step 2.

 UDL Insight

There are a number of UDL principles that are reflected in this activity, but the most important one is the goal of optimizing "relevance, value, and authenticity" (7.2). A well-developed thesis statement sets the tone for all of the thinking and writing that follows, and so My Human Thesis devotes instructional time to support students in the process of articulating thesis statements that reflect meaningful dimensions of their own lives (relevance), that they genuinely care about (value), and that spring from their own experiences and reflections (authenticity).

2. After having participated in this discussion, students should start thinking about their own research project. This step is intended to foster open-ended inquiry into the personal meanings that these research topics have for them. In true UDL spirit, students should be encouraged to pursue this inquiry in whatever way makes the most sense to them or is most likely to result in meaningful thinking.

Here is a sample of how the instructions for this step might sound:

PERSONAL REFLECTION EXAMPLE AND INSTRUCTIONS

Now that we know that there are aspects of existence that are uniquely human, how can we use these insights to "humanize" our own research projects?

For example:

I have chosen to research the lemurs of Madagascar. Why? I've never been to Madagascar, and I've only seen lemurs on television and at the zoo. Nevertheless, I find these lemurs interesting enough that I have decided to research them. There must be some personal connection that attracts me to this topic. If I can identify this personal connection, I can use it as the starting point for an original, meaningful, and human composition.

Some of my initial reflections look like this:

★ **My sense of self.** I've always felt a deep empathy with animals, especially primates, and I sometimes feel like learning new things about animals gives me insight into myself.

★ **My social and family relationships.** Lemur family groups remind me of my own large family, and sometimes family gatherings remind me of a huge lemur party.

★ **My memories of my past.** I remember watching the movie *Madagascar* with my siblings and thinking that the lemurs were my favorite characters.

★ **My hopes for my future.** I hope to own a business someday, and I wonder if lemur society can teach me anything about leadership, sustainability, and conflict resolution.

★ **My sense of justice and my moral values.** Deforestation and other threats to lemur habitats make me sad and outraged.

★ **My cultivation of physical and psychological wellness.** Looking at pictures of lemurs always seems to reduce my stress. Why are they so cute?

★ **My unconscious processes.** In a weird way, I think of lemurs as living in a kind of utopian community of natural order and happiness. I don't know if this is an accurate concept of lemur society, but I think that might be one of the things that attracts me to this topic.

After thinking through some of your initial reflections, choose one of these insights as the starting point for an introspective activity.

The activity may be any one of the following:

★ Talk to a friend/classmate.

★ Freewrite into your ideas.

★ Interview yourself in a podcast (or work with a friend/classmate and interview each other).

★ Create a collage of personal photos with captions explaining the photos' significance.

★ Sketch diagrams or drawings.

★ Write a haiku, slam poetry, or Dadaist free-association word cloud.

★ Literally anything else you can think of.

The purpose of the activity is simply to give you an opportunity to play around with the ideas that come out of the personal connections you are examining.

Challenge yourself to address yourself to this inquiry with honesty and rigor. See if you can surprise yourself by learning something new and possibly unexpected about yourself.

AI Aside

These days, it takes less than a minute for any computer to spit out a serviceable essay explaining the three types of rock, or containing three arguments for wearing seatbelts, or discussing the theme of power in *Moby-Dick*. Frustrated students are justified in asking, "If a computer can write this essay, then why should I have to do it? Isn't it a waste of my time, of my life, and of my unique cognitive potential to simply reproduce an essay that a computer could write much more quickly and, possibly, more effectively?" Taking this critique seriously provokes us to reimagine what student writing is for and what it can possibly become.

Rather than using writing assignments as a way of testing students on factual knowledge, or as a way of enforcing conformity with "robotic" conventions and tropes, we can make writing fully human for them. AI chatbots are very good at reprocessing things that have been written before by thousands of other people, but they are very bad at saying something new, and they are completely incapable of saying anything human. This activity encourages students to think about their thesis statements—the cornerstone of their compositions—through the lens of their own perspective and their own human experience. While this activity lends itself to writing that is more subjective and affect-oriented than is typical of conventional academic writing, it encourages students to engage in meaningful thinking and individual self-reflection. From this perspective, AI liberates student writers from the drudgery of rehashing shopworn ideas and launches them into new possibilities for using their writing to explore the things they have to say that no one else—biological or digital—has ever said or could ever say.

3. After having a chance to engage in the introspective activity, students should reconvene as a class and talk about their experience. If they have produced a composition (a poem, drawing, audio file, etc.), they can choose to either share it with the class or simply discuss their process.

The goals of this discussion should be to allow students to sum up the most meaningful insights from their introspective activity, to hear about how other students pursued their introspective inquiry, and to support and encourage one another.

At the same time, you can also use this activity to suggest strategies for students to develop some of these personal insights into thesis statements for more structured kinds of compositions.

As part of the discussion, each student should complete the following sentence:

Something that is really meaningful to me about my research topic is _____.

Examples:

Something that is really meaningful to me about my research topic is:

★ The way that lemurs take care of one another can teach human beings important lessons about kindness and decency.

★ The face of a lemur inspires an emotional response in humans that disrupts conventional attitudes about species boundaries.

★ The madcap lemur society represented in the film *Madagascar* may not be a scientifically accurate portrayal of lemur social organization, but it does provide a stunning satire of the irrationality, credulity, and groupthink that characterize many instances of human social organization.

Once students complete this prompt, they can cut off the prompt itself and, in many cases, be left with a thesis statement to use as the basis for an outline for their composition.

Composition Connection

While this activity obviously lends itself to developing compositions that are more personal or subjective, the prompt in step 3 suggests ways that this activity can generate thesis statements for more objective kinds of assignment as well. Even so-called objective compositions can benefit from being rooted in this extremely intimate form of introspective inquiry. Not only will students be more likely to identify angles on their research topics that align with their own networks of intrinsic motivation, but cultivating a personal sense of engagement with the topic makes all the information the student is working with "stickier"—that is, more deeply interwoven with the wider cognitive architecture of their unique brains.

ADDITIONAL SUGGESTIONS:

★ It may be helpful to expand step 3 to invite students to articulate more than one thesis that might emerge from their introspective analysis. If you are interested in having a class conversation about the relationship between more subjective and more objective styles of writing, you might ask students to develop thesis statements in both styles and then discuss how these open out into different kinds of compositions.

★ The thesis statements that students produce as the outcome of this assignment can become their starting point for the following two outlining activities.

Outsourcing Your Outline

Researchers sometimes get so bogged down in the details of their research projects that it can be difficult for them to achieve a clear sense of the big picture. This activity gives student researchers an opportunity to get outside perspectives on how they should organize their discussion of their topics, and it also gives the wider class community a chance to consider a range of strategies for structuring ideas into a linear sequence.

 UDL Overview

This outlining activity recruits the students' inherent diversity to examine how any given topic can be outlined in a variety of ways, as well as how a thesis statement can suggest a structural approach that might be particularly suitable. This activity provides options for comprehension—both of the body of information that individual students are working with and of the strategies and perspectives that go into the task of organizing information for an audience.

GOAL:

Provide students with personalized opportunities to practice and evaluate a variety of strategies for organizing information into rhetorical structures.

YOU WILL NEED:

A website or LMS for hosting students' research outline discussions

TIME:

Two or three class sessions

OUTCOMES:

Students will:

★ articulate a thesis statement for their writing project

- ★ develop rough outlines for a variety of thesis statements

- ★ apply conventional organizational strategies to the development of rough outlines

- ★ analyze thesis statements in terms of the rhetorical structures that might be used to elaborate them

- ★ compare the relative merits of multiple outlines

- ★ synthesize a variety of outline possibilities—including their own—into a single working outline for their writing project

DIRECTIONS:

1. The "entry ticket" for this activity is a thesis statement. Each student should produce a one-sentence statement encapsulating the main point of the writing project they have been working on.

   Students write their thesis statements onto a discussion board.

 UDL Insight

Asking students to write outlines for topics they have not researched activates background knowledge both about the topic and about outlining itself (3.1); discussing outlining ideas in small groups and as a whole class highlights "patterns, critical features, big ideas, and relationships" (3.2); the conversation about students' outlines supports students as they process information (3.3); and the emphasis on how a few simple outlining strategies can apply to a wide variety of topics maximizes students' ability to generalize these techniques (3.4). In short, the Outsourcing Your Outline project runs the table on the "comprehension" box of the UDL chart.

2. Conduct a mini-lesson or class discussion about outlining strategies. Students might start by brainstorming the strategies they use when they are organizing material for a writing project, and then you can compile their ideas into a list of best practices and helpful tips.

   This class discussion should include key strategies such as:

   ★ chunking together similar subtopics

   ★ arranging information from more obvious/general to more speculative/specific

   ★ applying conventional rhetorical structures such as:

   ★ narrative/chronology

   ★ claim–arguments

   ★ problem–solution

   ★ comparison/contrast

   ★ combinations of these structures

   As a class, brainstorm a random thesis statement and practice collaboratively outlining an essay arising from this thesis statement from scratch, applying the practices discussed in the mini-lesson.

3. After the mini-lesson, divide the class into working groups of three, and one student either volunteers or is randomly chosen to outsource their outline. This means that each student group locates that student's thesis on the discussion board and works together to develop an outline for a potential essay built on that thesis statement.

   Depending on the assignment, students in the class may know something about the topic addressed by the thesis statement (in which case this activity provides an engaging opportunity to review course content), but it is not necessary that students know anything about the topic. In fact, this activity works well when students are working on far-flung individual research projects about which their classmates may have only limited knowledge. Students who lack expertise in the area covered by the thesis statement are able to consider the structural question from an outsider's point of view. They are situated in a way that aligns their perspective with that of a possible reader, someone who doesn't know much about the topic but is eager to learn.

Students should be dissuaded from doing any "phone research" on the topics they're outlining, concentrating instead on questions of structure and on their own expectations as readers.

Critical questions to guide their outlining process include:

★ What will the writer need to explain?

★ What kind of information will this writer likely be citing?

★ What kind of rhetorical structure do I expect to follow from this thesis statement (a story, an argument, a description, etc.)?

★ What would the writer need to do in order to fulfill the expectations raised by this thesis statement?

The outcome of this activity should be a rough outline, a list of at least five subtopics indicating how the student group would structure an essay based on the sample thesis statement. Each subtopic can be thought of as the main point of a body paragraph.

Groups should post their outlines as responses to the thesis statement on the discussion board.

During this time, the student who supplied the sample thesis statement can work with their own group, but they might also make themselves available to the rest of the class as a "roaming expert" capable of answering questions about the topic.

 **AI Aside**

For an AI twist on this assignment, invite the student groups to ask a chatbot to write a five-paragraph essay based on the thesis statement they're working with. How did the chatbot organize its essay? Did it use any of the strategies discussed in the mini-lesson? How would you evaluate the effectiveness of the chatbot's organization of its essay?

4. After all the groups have posted their rough outlines to the discussion board, you and the student who supplied the sample thesis statement should co-facilitate a discussion about the groups' response to this outlining challenge. As each student group presents their outline and describes their process, you can identify techniques that the groups used to develop their outlines: identifying relevant information, breaking down the topic into component parts, locating relationships among the different parts, and sequencing the parts into a complete rhetorical structure.

Comparing the different student outlines is also an ideal opportunity to consider the way that a single idea can unfold in different directions, and to evaluate these variations in terms of how effectively they demonstrate the thesis. This conversation also might reveal areas of uniformity across the groups, which may indicate that certain expectations are built in to a thesis statement.

5. If possible, repeat steps 3 and 4 until every student in the class has a chance to have their outline outsourced.

6. In a follow-up discussion board post (text, video, or audio), students reflect on how they feel about outlining their own essay after having

reviewed the different outlines produced by the student groups. Suggested questions include:

★ Did the groups' ideas correspond with your own?

★ Did they suggest new perspectives that you hadn't considered?

★ Is there one of these outlines that sounds right for you?

These reflections should accompany the student's own five-part rough outline for their own composition.

ADDITIONAL SUGGESTIONS:

★ This activity can be telescoped to adapt to different levels of detail. On the one hand, writing very rough five-part outlines allows students to focus on big structural questions, and also to move through one another's thesis statements more briskly. On the other hand, inviting students to take more time and to make their outlines more elaborate—introducing, for example, subordinated subtopics for each main point— can be a way of looking at the finer-grained structures of individual paragraphs.

★ To help bridge the gap between outlining and drafting, consider having the groups phrase their main point in the form of a topic sentence for a body paragraph.

★ In the absence of an LMS, this activity can be done analog style, with students writing their thesis on the whiteboard, and student groups writing their rough outlines on sticky notes and posting them to the board.

Index Card Shuffle

Once upon a time, index cards enjoyed a significant place in the researcher's toolkit. Recording relevant nuggets of information on index cards allowed researchers not only to keep track of these details but also to play around with how these details were grouped and sequenced. Arranging and rearranging the index cards suggested different organizational opportunities for researchers as they began shaping their findings into paragraphs and blocks of paragraphs. This activity invites students to rediscover this bygone but useful technique.

 UDL Connection

Word processing technology is wonderful, but the frame of the scrolling digital screen can sometimes make it difficult for writers to conceptualize the larger structural issues that play an important role in composition. This activity pulls students out of the digital writing environment and gives them a haptic, visual, and manipulable tool for considering various options for finding connections among different elements of a writing project. The activity also involves opportunities for students both to work through their own ideas about their outlines and also to discuss their ideas with classmates, making connections between interpersonal communication and textual composition.

GOAL:

Involve students in strategies for organizing specific pieces of information into larger rhetorical structures.

YOU WILL NEED:

Index cards. A lot of them.

TIME:

Two or three class sessions

OUTCOMES:

Students will:

- ★ identify relevant information from a piece of writing and from their own research notes

- ★ discuss and implement connective strategies for explaining the relationships among different pieces of information

- ★ assemble discrete pieces of information into rhetorical structures

- ★ evaluate different strategies for sequencing and clustering discrete pieces of information

- ★ explain their reasoning for their outlining decisions

- ★ answer critical questions about the content and organization of a developing writing project

- ★ produce a working outline for a developing writing project

DIRECTIONS

1. This activity begins with a "practice scramble" as a way of examining the relationship between the parts and the whole of a piece of writing. Identify a sample composition. It could be a student essay or a professional article, but it should be something that the student has not read before.

   Divide the class into two halves. The first half are the Analysts, and the second group are the Synthesists. If possible, the two groups should separate into two separate rooms.

   The Analysts' job is to read the writing sample and to comb through it for specific details that can be recorded on an index card. Elements may include:

   - ★ a quote

   - ★ a statistic

- ★ a chart or graph
- ★ an opinion
- ★ a fact
- ★ a story
- ★ an observation
- ★ a definition

The group can assign different members to be responsible for individual paragraphs, with every member responsible for coming up with two or three index cards. The goal should be 20 index cards, each one containing some element from the article. There is no need for the index cards to comprehensively cover the entire essay; rather, each card should isolate some particular detail, but there should be details from every part of the essay.

As the group generates the cards, they should keep track of the sequence in which the elements recorded on the cards appear in the writing sample. The Analysts record the sequence of cards, but then scramble them.

Now it is the Synthesists' turn. Their job is to attempt to organize the index cards in a way that makes them fit together into a story; the goal is not necessarily to guess the "right" order, but to put these details together in a way that makes sense to them. The group should be able to talk through the deck of cards, making connections from one card to the next.

2. Have the groups reconvene and discuss their process.

First, the Synthesists should talk through the deck of cards, making connections from one card to the next and explaining their reasoning for organizing the cards the way they did.

Then, the Analysts describe how the Synthesists' reconstruction compares with the original writing sample.

Similarities and divergences between the two outlines are both instructive for what they reveal about strategies for clumping ideas into patterns and structures. The conversation should focus on the kinds of "connective tissue" that writers use to forge connection between different pieces of information, such as:

- ★ cause–effect
- ★ paradigm–example
- ★ claim–evidence
- ★ problem–solution
- ★ beginning–middle–end
- ★ continua of intensity or severity

The goal of this conversation should be to equip student writers with ways of thinking about how individual pieces of information can be assembled into larger rhetorical structures. Optimally, students perceive how these rhetorical structures are prefabricated to a certain extent but also highly manipulable.

 UDL Insight

This activity invites students to "use multiple tools for construction and composition" (5.2), not only in using index cards to supplement the digital manipulation of information, but also in encouraging students to include different types of content on their index cards and in allowing students the chance to think through structural issues in different interpersonal contexts: as part of a half-class team, in a whole-class discussion, in pairs, and in independent self-reflection. These social arrangements can be thought of as a variety of tools that enable students to think about rhetorical structure from multiple perspectives.

3. For homework: After participating in the group activity and discussion, students now turn to their own research notes for their ongoing composition project. Challenge students to identify elements from their own research and thinking that they intend to include in their composition. These can be specific quotations or pieces of data, but they can also be personal impressions, interpretations, or ideas. Students write each element down on an individual index card, and they should try to come up with at least 20 cards.

Now, students can practice the "synthetic" techniques discussed in step 2. Challenge them to arrange the cards in a way that allows them to talk about each element in a linear sequence. They should consider the connective tissue that links each card to the next and play around with the order until they find a storyline that makes sense to them and is easy for them to explain. They should also feel free to sideline cards that don't seem to fit into their storyline.

 AI Aside

In addition to combing through their research notes, students may also consult a chatbot to help them find facts, quotes, definitions, statistics, and so forth related to their research topics to include on their index cards.

4. Back in class: Split students up into pairs. One student in each pair talks through their deck of index cards, telling the story that connects the individual elements.

Following the student's narrative, the student's partner responds with feedback, describing what parts of the story fit together in an intuitive way and what parts of the story were less clear.

The student pairs can also discuss the following questions:

★ If you had to take out a card, which would it be?

- ★ If you had to take out half the cards, which ones would they be?
- ★ If you had to reduce your deck to three cards, which cards would you keep (and why)?
- ★ What does the first card do? Why is it different from all the other cards?
- ★ What does the last card do? Why is it different from all of the other cards?
- ★ Divide your deck into three subpiles. Where are the divisions?
- ★ Does your partner have any suggestions for new cards to add?

After the pair has had a chance to talk through the first student's index card deck, the students switch hats and the second student gets a chance to talk through their deck, narrating their story and addressing the same questions.

 Composition Connection

Outlining is generally considered a solitary enterprise, but writing is an inherently social activity at every level, from the other researchers whose work the writer is building on to the future readers who are the audience for the piece of writing. Inviting students to discuss their works in progress with their classmates emphasizes the storytelling nature of writing, requiring students to consider the crucial question of why someone else should be interested in what they have to say, and also to practice techniques for attracting and retaining their interest. When students describe their writing projects to other students, they intuitively employ rhetorical and structural strategies that can be directly incorporated into their essays.

5. Once students have arrived at a deck arrangement that makes sense to them, they can transcribe the content of the cards into a word processing document. This series of items can now serve as an outline for their composition. This outline should also include the connective links that clarify the arrangement of details.

ADDITIONAL SUGGESTIONS:

★ The index cards that the students generate from their own notes do not have to be exclusively textual. Encourage students to record their ideas about their writing project in whatever form makes sense to them. They can print out pictures, memes, or charts and glue them to cards; sketch their own diagrams or drawings; include mathematical formulas; or use their index cards in any other way they can imagine.

★ In an online class, you could replace the decks of index cards with PowerPoint presentations. Virtual index cards offer the advantage of being able to include links and other digital content (but PowerPoint slides are harder and a lot less fun to scramble).

★ As an alternative to working in pairs, students can record videos of themselves talking through their narrative and addressing the questions in step 4.

Drafting

The drafting stage of the writing process presents unique instructional challenges. To me, it sometimes sounds like a set of instructions to build an elephant that goes like this:

1. *Think about the elephant you want to build.*
2. *Research what elephants look like.*
3. *Plan your elephant.*
4. *Build your elephant.*
5. *Ride the elephant.*

There's something about step 4 that makes it different from the others. For writing students, thinking about drafting as one step in a wider process certainly helps reduce the challenge of producing a first draft, but, at some point, students actually have to sit down and start articulating sentences and paragraphs, a moment that can be intimidating even for the most accomplished and prolific writers.

One of the reasons why drafting sentences and paragraphs can be so challenging is that, in a situation where textual writing is the required outcome, a writer's "options for expression" bottleneck down to a single medium. This book embraces the many different ways that there are to brainstorm ideas, gather information, and organize rhetorical structures, but writers at a keyboard often feel trapped into performing an activity that they don't know how to do. All the open-ended possibilities that their imagination had entertained about their ideas and impressions suddenly have to be marshaled through a narrow gap, in a single-file stream of letters and words, and it is not surprising when students feel that this task is just as impossible as building an elephant.

One time-honored solution that students employ to resolve this dilemma is plagiarism. If they can borrow from someone who has already done the work of translating their ideas into words and sentences, then their elephant comes prefabricated. The updated variant of this strategy, the AI chatbot solution, may seem less ethically problematic since it's not generally perceived as an act of intellectual theft, and one could even argue that the chatbot's response to your own prompt is an expression of original work. One could also argue that cutting and pasting passages from other writers into a plagiarized text-collage is also an expression of originality (and maybe even an interesting process-oriented writing activity). But in these cases, a crucial element of the writing situation is undermined: the moment of articulation, the point at which writers find the words for what they mean.

For many writing instructors, this is the heart and soul of writing itself, not only because it results in a certain outcome (a piece of textual writing) but also because it represents a kind of existential encounter between the writer, language, and ideas. It becomes an encounter where ideas are not only expressed but often generated, elaborated, and positioned into place. Indeed, there are many other expressive media that human beings use to provoke these kinds of existential encounters, but writing is definitely one of them, and one that obviously holds particular relevance in academic and professional work, and especially in a writing class. Although different students will certainly have different preferences and aptitudes when it comes to expressing themselves, developing confidence as textual writers can empower students to rise to the impossible challenge of building their elephant, and even to feel motivated and liberated by the very impossibility itself. Drafting sentences onto an empty screen is like leaping off into a void, but students who feel supported to take that leap of faith discover that they can fly.

All of the activities in this handbook can be thought of as ways of trying to fill the void of the empty screen with ideas, perspectives, and plans, or, to switch back to the other metaphor, to supply genetic material for the elephant. The activities that follow all share the outcome of supporting students as they draft out written text, but they use a variety of other media to embed the drafting process in modes of expression that may be more spontaneous and familiar. Students work collaboratively, in discussion, under low-stakes conditions, and supported by multimedia frameworks to build bridges between oral or interpersonal fluency and written fluency. These UDL-based strategies explore the ways in which multimodal forms of composition can provide a framework for composing in the "monomodal" medium of textual writing.

Collaborative Paragraph Drafting

In professional contexts, writers frequently work in teams. Collaborative writing situations can enrich writing by weaving together multiple perspectives, and they can also provide opportunities for different writers to think metacognitively about the shared conventions and values that bring them together. This activity fosters collaborative writing as both a community-building exercise and as a way of thinking through the structural maneuvers that make a paragraph a socially recognized unit of meaning.

 UDL Overview

UDL pedagogy celebrates learner variability not only as an inevitable component of any educational setting, but also as an educational resource. This collaborative writing exercise provides a vivid example of an activity that brings together students' different vocabularies, perspectives, and areas of expertise to work toward a common purpose.

GOAL:

Support students as they identify and implement structural solutions in the composition of textual paragraphs.

YOU WILL NEED:

A website or LMS for hosting student outlines and paragraph drafts.

TIME:

Two or three class sessions

OUTCOMES:

Students will:

- ★ identify a section of their research paper outline that is ready for drafting
- ★ analyze the structural elements of an academic body paragraph
- ★ work collaboratively in both whole-class and breakout-group settings to compose sentences and paragraphs
- ★ assess the effectiveness of collaboratively written paragraphs
- ★ apply information about the structural elements of paragraphs to the drafting process

DIRECTIONS:

1. As the starting point for this assignment, each student needs to have formulated an outline for a research paper. They should identify a section of this outline that is particularly well developed and that contains material for a potential body paragraph.

   Based on this material, each student should:

   a. Articulate a topic sentence for the proposed body paragraph.

   b. Provide two or three bullet points for supporting details that this paragraph may include (quotes, facts, statistics, arguments, etc.).

Each student should post this paragraph outline to an LMS discussion board.

 AI Aside

One of the reasons AI programs are able to write convincing paragraphs is because they know the formulaic structure that paragraphs are built around. This activity puts students in the position of a text-generating AI program: they need to take a random topic and some basic information and shape this material into a paragraph. The fact that this job can be done so readily by a computer program may demystify the process, revealing the composition of paragraphs to be little more than the application of a few simple rules. This activity gives students a chance to discover these rules and to experiment with putting them into practice.

2. As a whole class, pick one of the students' paragraph outlines and work together to compose it into a textual paragraph. Using the topic sentence as a starting point, facilitate the collaborative effort to develop further sentences along a formulaic sequence that may look something like this:

   ★ a sentence that follows up on the topic sentence

   ★ a sentence that links to the first subpoint

   ★ a sentence that articulates the first subpoint

   ★ a sentence that links to the second subpoint

   ★ ...

   ★ a concluding sentence that expresses a sense of closure

The students might be challenged to write out their own version of such sentences and then share them with the class, who can then discuss the relative merits of the students' different versions and synthesize them into agreed-upon final versions. You should type out the paragraph draft as it emerges sentence by sentence from the collaborative process.

After the collaborative paragraph is posted in the discussion board, give the students an opportunity to reflect on the quality of the final version of the paragraph, and maybe even to copy and paste the paragraph into a response post in order to implement their own editorial suggestions.

3. Split students up into groups of three and randomly assign each group one of the outline segments from the discussion board. The group works together to develop this outline segment into a complete body paragraph using the same structural principles employed during the whole-class activity.

Some ground rules:

- ★ Every group member should participate in the drafting process (rather than letting one member of the group write out the whole paragraph). One strategy might be for each member of the group to try drafting the paragraph individually, and then compare their versions and weave them into a single final version.

- ★ Student groups should not do any research as they write their paragraphs. They should rely on what is in the outline segment and whatever general knowledge they have about the topic.

- ★ The paragraphs should be at least seven sentences long.

When students are done composing their paragraphs, they can post them as a response to the discussion board comment containing the original outline segment.

UDL Insight

One UDL Guideline that this activity is particularly focused on addressing is 5.3: "Build fluencies with graduated levels of support for practice and performance." Process-oriented writing instruction typically provides support for students as they work through the prewriting, research, and revision stages, but the drafting itself—which can be one of the most challenging parts of the writing process—is frequently assigned as a task that the students do on their own. Progress from whole-class instruction to small-group work to individual assignments allows student writers to practice drafting strategies in a supportive environment that embraces different levels of confidence and expertise.

4. The class reconvenes to review the paragraphs composed by the small groups. For each collaboratively written paragraph, the small group who composed the paragraph can talk about:

   ★ challenges they experienced and how they worked through them

   ★ their impressions of the quality of the finished paragraph

   ★ their suggestions for further elaboration and revision

   The student whose outline served as the basis for the paragraph can talk about:

   ★ how closely the collaboratively written paragraph matches up with or deviates from their own ideas about how this paragraph should be composed

- ★ what other information from the student's research might help to enhance this paragraph

- ★ how much of this paragraph the student intends to use in the research paper draft that they will compose

You can talk about:

- ★ technical revisions that might enhance the professionalism and "polish" of the drafted paragraph

- ★ how to cite quotes or other information contained in the paragraph

- ★ suggestions for connecting this paragraph to the student writer's thesis and for positioning it within the structure of the emerging draft

Steps 3 and 4 can be repeated until all students get a chance to have one of their paragraphs drafted out.

 Composition Connection

Composing academic prose involves a mixture of personal and impersonal perspectives. As important as it is to feel personally engaged in and connected to a topic you're writing about, sometimes these feelings can interfere with the "cooler" calculations that writers have to perform in order to write sentences that make sense to other people. By temporarily removing the writer-researcher from the drafting situation, this activity draws students' attention to these structural elements underlying the drafting process.

5. Using the collaboratively written paragraph as a stub, and applying the drafting strategies practiced in the whole-class and small-group portions of this activity, students draft out the other paragraphs of the research paper they are working on.

ADDITIONAL SUGGESTIONS:

★ As students revise the collaboratively written paragraphs at the end of step 2 and in step 5, you may encourage them to use a "track changes" tool to record their revisions. Doing so not only makes it easier for their classmates to see the edits they made, but also provides an educational opportunity for students to become familiar with this useful feature.

★ The obvious next step for this assignment is to instruct students to use the same drafting techniques that they used to draft their classmates' paragraphs to draft out the rest of the body paragraphs for their own research paper.

★ A similar activity can support students as they master strategies for composing introductory and concluding paragraphs, but, in these cases, the "formula" outlined in step 2 is very different, an insight that may open up thoughtful conversations about the different forms and functions of different kinds of paragraphs.

Scripting an Instructional Video

The genre of the research paper can intimidate and alienate students who might find it an unfamiliar or onerous medium. This activity uses a genre that is likely to be more familiar to students—the video lecture—as a framework to help them not only draft out their textual research papers but also explore the ways that multimedia forms of expression can complement and inform one another.

📄 UDL Overview

This project is primarily inspired by UDL principle II: provide multiple means of action and expression. For obvious reasons, writing classes tend to focus on writing as the central form of expression. By embedding the writing assignment within the audiovisual context of a lecture video, however, this project encourages students to make connections between their writing and other media of self-expression. At the same time, the multimedia nature of the final product allows for multiple means of assessment to supplement the class's focus on written composition.

GOAL:

Provide students with support and guidance as they work through the process of drafting a research paper.

YOU WILL NEED:

★ presentation software and audio recording equipment

★ a website or LMS for hosting student slideshows and videos

TIME:

Four or five class sessions

OUTCOMES:

Students will:

★ develop a PowerPoint slideshow to communicate their ideas about a research topic

- ★ deliver a PowerPoint presentation to classmates
- ★ respond to suggestions and implement editorial suggestions into revised versions of their presentations
- ★ script out ideas presented in oral form into text
- ★ revise textual writing to enhance its level of formality and adherence to academic conventions
- ★ record a narration for an instructional video
- ★ produce and publish an instructional video
- ★ develop a draft for a research paper based on their process of developing an oral presentation and instructional video
- ★ respond supportively and constructively to the work of their classmates

 Composition Connection

Whereas traditional writing classes emphasize the centrality of the word processing program as the predominant and often exclusive "tool" for composition, the sequence of assignments leading up to the video lecture requires students to articulate their ideas through a range of media tools, including oral reporting, structured discussion, visual imagery, and, of course, video. More importantly, the fluidity of the relationship among these different media of expression (the reflection essays inform the small-group discussions, which evolve into a PowerPoint presentation, which develops into an essay, which becomes a video, and so on) fosters an awareness of their interconnections and relative strengths and weaknesses.

DIRECTIONS:

1. If students have already developed an outline for their research composition, that can become the basis for a deck of PowerPoint slides. In this step, they translate each of the outline's major points into a slide, which may include images, texts, diagrams and charts, or any combination of elements. The important thing is that each slide provides an opportunity for the student to discuss that particular part of the outline.

   If students have not yet developed an outline for their research composition, they can use this step as an opportunity to organize their ideas in the form of a slideshow lecture.

 AI Aside

Many AI chatbots also generate PowerPoint presentations based on topics, outlines, or scripts. This activity gives students a chance to experiment with this functionality in a way that allows the classroom community to evaluate the quality of AI-generated slideshows and to suggest strategies for editing and personalizing them.

2. Once the students have developed their slideshows, the next step is to deliver their presentation to their classmates. It is important to emphasize that, unlike many of the other presentations they may have given in previous classes, this presentation is not meant to be a finished product. This presentation is merely a chance for students to try out the organizational structure sketched out in their outlines and to talk through their ideas about their research topic in front of a supportive audience of colleagues. The purpose of the presentation is not to articulate the final word on the research topic, but rather to

get a feel for how the ideas stick together, which parts of the student outlines make sense to them, and which parts of their discussions might need more support or development.

It may be worth devoting a few class sessions to this stage of the assignment so that every student gets a chance not only to deliver their presentation but also to receive feedback from classmates about what they understood, what they were confused about, what other information or perspectives might be included, and which parts of the presentation might be cut out or whittled down.

The experience of delivering their remarks before the class allows students to identify awkward, repetitive, and underdeveloped elements in their own arguments. At the same time, the opportunity to respond supportively to their classmates' presentations provides a chance to discuss best practices related to oral presentations and to identify successful strategies and techniques related to this genre. The classroom community can also compare different students' organizational strategies, identify common challenges that students are encountering, and brainstorm solutions to particular rhetorical or structural questions suggested by students' presentations.

 UDL Insight

The graduated nature of this activity allows students to "build fluencies with graduated levels of support for practice and performance" (5.3). The low-stakes assignments toward the beginning of the sequence allow the students (and you as well) to develop an awareness of their strengths as writers and to identify specific areas for continued improvement. The progressive organization of the assignments steadily raises the degree of complexity with each stage, building new elements on previous stages in a way that exemplifies the principle of scaffolded instruction.

3. Once these presentations have been delivered and revised, students "script them out" into complete sentences and paragraphs. Drafting is typically the most challenging part of the writing process for most students, who often feel alone in their attempts to connect their ideas into a coherent piece of writing. Reconceptualizing this stage of the process as scripting out a presentation that they have already designed and delivered, however, helps the students proceed more confidently, having received support from both you and the class in developing and organizing their arguments.

   If they would like, students can record their presentations and use speech-to-text tools to generate a transcript that can work as the starting point for this draft. Now that they already know what they need to say to explain each slide, they can simply try to express these ideas in the more formal language of prepared text.

   A tip that will help students with this process is to encourage them to think of each slide in their presentation as a paragraph in their script. Each discussion of each new slide should begin with a topic sentence that introduces the main point of the slide, followed by more granular discussion of the slide's contents.

4. Work with individual students to evaluate the transcripts for technical fluency, factual accuracy, and rhetorical effectiveness. Once each student has a chance to participate in this editorial process, they are cleared to begin recording narrated video versions of their presentations, reading the script from step 3 along with the slideshow from step 1.

   In addition to supplementing the visual aspect of written communication with the oral aspect of spoken communication, reading one's own writing aloud is a valuable editing strategy that this stage of the video project encourages students to practice. The challenge of recording their scripts into a video lecture focuses students' attention on the sound of their language. In addition to scanning for issues related to the organization and development of their ideas, students are also encouraged to reflect on how to make their sentences clearer and their meaning more accessible.

The recording sessions also invite reflection on the art of elocution and timing. Commonly, students tend to read too fast or to read through sentences without being clear about their meaning. Between "takes" of the recording session, students can work together to specify places where the reader should pause for breath or mark specific words and phrases that merit emphasis. The opportunity to record multiple takes fosters a low-stakes environment where students are able to refine their oral delivery in ways that enhance the clarity of their presentation and practice strategies for reading and speaking clearly and effectively.

5. Once the students have recorded the videos, they can post them on the LMS. Students can respond to one another's finished videos on the discussion board, and those who are willing to share their work with the rest of the world can post their videos on YouTube or share them through other personal social media channels.

At the same time, the script that students develop for this project can become the draft of a research paper. The script may need further revisions to stand alone as a research paper, but these revisions should not be too difficult to implement, and working to identify them is an opportunity to discuss the general differences between a PowerPoint script and a research paper.

ADDITIONAL SUGGESTIONS:

★ This activity plan refers to PowerPoint presentations, but students can use many other styles of presentation software to support their presentations and videos. PowerPoint is a useful reference due to its familiarity and accessibility, but you can encourage students to experiment with other platforms.

★ When students complete their research paper, they can post it on an accessible web-based platform and provide a link in the description of their YouTube video, or brainstorm other ways of cross-promoting their paper and their video together as a multimedia bundle.

★ In an online class, students can record their improvised voiceover directly to a slideshow video and share the videos in an LMS discussion board that can then host the community feedback conversation from step 2. Some students in a face-to-face class might also prefer to present their oral presentations as prerecorded videos, in which case you should invite them to do so.

Research Roundup Podcast

Guest activity by Dana Sheehan

Research is a conversation—or rather, several conversations that all overlap with one another. It is a conversation with other researchers, one with yourself, and one with curious learners who want to benefit from your insights. This activity invites students to participate in this conversation, positioning them as experts in their research field and helping them connect their conversational voice to their authorial writing voice.

 UDL Overview

UDL theory celebrates the many different modalities of self-expression and the proliferation of new media. As podcasts have become a popular form of disseminating information and ideas, educators have been finding ways to incorporate podcasts into their classes as both a source of information and an alternative format for students to articulate their own perspectives. In this activity, the podcast genre—with its conversational, semi-spontaneous, and aural-oral characteristics—presents an opportunity for writing students to collect their thoughts, reflect on what they have to say, communicate their ideas to another person and to an anonymous audience of listeners, and use their spoken words as a starting point for their writing.

GOAL:

Help students practice strategies for developing oral forms of self-expression into textual forms.

YOU WILL NEED:

Audio recording equipment and editing software

TIME:

Four or five class sessions

OUTCOMES:

Students will:

- ★ formulate interview questions about another student's research project
- ★ formulate responses from another student about their own research project
- ★ conduct a recorded oral interview of a fellow student
- ★ answer questions about their research project in a recorded oral interview
- ★ edit, produce, and post a podcast episode
- ★ provide feedback to fellow students about their podcast episodes
- ★ assess the podcast transcript for elements that can be repurposed as material for a written composition
- ★ assemble elements of the podcast transcript into a working draft for a research paper

DIRECTIONS:

1. Pair students up with a partner. Once they have met their partner, the two students should have an unstructured conversation where they get to know each other (if they don't already) and learn about

each other's research. There is no need to go into too much detail at this point; the goal is simply for each student to get a general sense of what their partner is researching.

2. Following the initial conversation between partners, reconvene the entire class and introduce the podcast interview assignment. As part of the drafting process, the pairs of students will record interviews with their partners and produce them as podcasts. Each student will be the producer of their own episode featuring the interview with their partner.

The class can come up with their own name for their podcast series. A default option can be "Research Roundup."

Ask students to recall interviews that they have seen and heard on television, radio, and digital media, and to formulate best practices for conducting a recorded or live interview, such as:

★ Be prepared with questions.

★ Do some research of your own to acquire background knowledge and context.

★ Listen carefully.

★ Use follow-up questions to pursue interesting points or clarify details.

The class might also brainstorm standard interview questions that may help student interviewers think through the process of writing their own questions, such as:

★ What are the goals of your research?

★ Provide an overview of the topic you are researching for people who might not know anything about it.

★ What is the most interesting thing you've learned as a result of your research?

★ Why do you think your research is important?

Supplement the discussion of these stock interview questions with a discussion about the value of formulating specific questions that address issues and ideas related to the research itself.

 AI Aside

One helpful way to take advantage of AI chatbots in this lesson is for students to ask a digital assistant to suggest interview questions relating to their partner's research topic. A chatbot can quickly generate a response to a prompt like, "10 interview questions about mental health in prisons." Some of the responses may be totally irrelevant, some may be productively thought-provoking, and others might be combined or edited in ways that support the students' process of identifying appropriate questions to ask their partners. This use of AI in the composition process exemplifies how AI tools can help support, rather than replace, thinking.

3. Students now write a list of interview questions to ask their partner.

For the purposes of this assignment, the questions should focus on the research rather than the researcher. The interview questions should provide the student researchers with a chance to describe and explain what they have learned.

Six or seven questions will probably be sufficient. This step might be assigned as homework.

>  **UDL Insight**
>
> This activity is inspired primarily by UDL Guideline 5.2, "Use multiple tools for construction and composition," since the oral-audio component of the podcast interview supports the composition of the textual draft. But it also addresses several other UDL Guidelines, including "Foster collaboration and community" (8.3), "Offer alternatives for visual information" (1.3), and "Develop self-assessment and reflection" (9.3).

4. Students share their interview questions with their partners. Each student should have a block of time, perhaps an entire class period, to think about how they want to answer the questions and maybe even to sketch out notes detailing points they want to make, relevant research that they can refer to in their interview, and specific phrases or remarks that they want to have at hand. Students can compile these notes individually, as a whole class, or as some combination thereof.

5. Students record their podcasts. This may take a few class sessions. If students can break up into separate rooms, they will likely be able to record their interviews using their own laptops or phones. Each pair of students should record two separate interviews, one where Student A is the interviewee and Student B is the interviewer, and then a second interview where the roles are reversed. Encourage students to record their interviews all the way through without stopping.

If students wish to do so, they should be encouraged to take some time to edit their audio files to cut out flubbed lines or dead air. You may also provide intro music that students can add in the beginning to standardize the podcasts and make them sound more professional. They should also give their episode a number and a descriptive title that identifies the research topic under discussion (e.g., Research Roundup, Episode 5: "Mental Health in Prisons").

6. Students post their podcasts onto an LMS discussion board. Each student picks three of their classmates' podcasts to listen to, based on their interest in the various research topics. In a discussion board response, each student should respond to the following prompt for each podcast that they listen to:

   ★ After listening to your classmate's podcast, what advice do you have about how the researcher might shape what they have to say into a research paper? Consider some of the following questions (you do not have to answer every question for each podcast that you listen to, but you are welcome to do so):

      ★ Does this researcher seem to have a "thesis"? If so, what is it?

      ★ What was the most interesting thing that the researcher said?

      ★ What did the writer say that might provide material for the introductory paragraph of a research paper?

      ★ What did the researcher say that might provide material for the concluding paragraph of a research paper?

   Responding to such questions gives students a chance both to provide practical advice to their classmates and to think through how some of the same structural issues relate to their own work.

7. Students can now use this feedback and their own reflections to shape what they said during the podcast interview into a draft for a research paper. A voice-to-text transcript program can produce a written transcript of the students' podcast remarks, which can be mined, edited, rearranged, and supplemented to produce the draft.

   It is important to emphasize that the drafts that emerge from this process will likely be very patchy. While there might be passages from the interview that can be translated verbatim into research paper text, it is likely that the document that emerges from this process may look more like a cross between an outline and a draft, with some sections filled in with text and other sections simply listing topics that either didn't come up in the interview or weren't discussed in any detail. This is okay. The point is just to get started. Once the "draft line" is in place, students can continue shaping and developing it into a more formal expression of their ideas.

ADDITIONAL SUGGESTIONS:

★ Students who would feel more comfortable working alone than with a partner should have the opportunity to do so. They can write their own questions and interview themselves. Students who miss class on the first day of this lesson can also take advantage of this option.

★ If students consent to have their podcast published online, you can make the series of podcasts available on a podcast platform for a worldwide audience, possibly accompanied by links to online versions of their final research papers.

★ For online classes, it might be easier for the student teams to record a video-chat session of their interview with their partners, instead of trying to capture the audio alone. These video chats can then be edited, transcribed, and posted as a video interview rather than as a podcast.

AI-Informed Drafting

The chatbots are among us. Writing students will inevitably be availing themselves of increasingly sophisticated AI programs as part of their composition process, and the question is not whether or not writing instructors will permit them to do so, but how we can guide students to use this technology in a way that enhances their writing rather than causes them to "write themselves out" of their own educational experience. This activity describes a process that many writers have already found themselves employing in the post-chatbot world: using chatbot input as a research partner and "sous-writer" who takes care of the grunt work of collating generic facts about a topic and frees the human writer to do the human work of making that information meaningful.

 UDL Overview

In the context of composition instruction, chatbots can be thought of as an assistive technology that can make writing more accessible, specifically for students who face diagnosed physical, cognitive, or social-emotional challenges in educational settings, but also for anyone who struggles with the complex task of writing, which includes just about all of us. The UDL Guidelines encourage instructors to empower students to "use multiple tools for construction and composition," and chatbots are a tool that can help a wide variety of students in a wide variety of ways, serving as a virtual writing tutor, research assistant, editor, and brainstorming companion.

GOAL:

Encourage students to use chatbot-generated responses responsibly and thoughtfully as a part of their own writing process.

YOU WILL NEED:

Access to ChatGPT or another chatbot platform

TIME:

Two class sessions

OUTCOMES:

Students will:

- ★ articulate chatbot prompts that define the agenda of their research projects
- ★ evaluate and assess writing composed by chatbots
- ★ compare AI-generated text with their expectations for their own writing
- ★ analyze the literary characteristics of AI-generated text
- ★ identify opportunities for building on AI-generated text with their own insights and observations
- ★ use chatbot technology in constructive ways to facilitate their own writing process

 UDL Insight

This activity uses students' responses to chatbot text as a way of engaging them in the process of thinking more deeply about their own writing and, indeed, their own humanity. This line of inquiry invites students to play an active role in optimizing the "relevance, value, and authenticity" (7.2) of the writing they are doing in the class. As they compare their own thinking with the chatbot's, they practice a unique form of "self-assessment and reflection" that speaks to fundamental questions about their identity as learners, thinkers, and language users.

DIRECTIONS:

1. As students are beginning to draft out their papers, challenge them to see if they can get a chatbot to write their paper for them. Tell

them not to pull any punches. They should do their best to feed a prompt into the chatbot that details the specifications of their own writing project, including the thesis, the target word count, and any other features that the desired final paper should have (supporting research, main points from the outline, etc.). Encourage students to continue refining the chatbot prompt in an effort to generate a paper that's as close as possible to the one they are planning to write.

It may be helpful to try to work as a whole class with one or two sample student papers in order to coach students through strategies for articulating prompts that will generate the desired output. In addition to the immediate result of producing the AI-generated version of the students' papers, the process of articulating and refining their prompts provides an opportunity for students to think through their expectations for their own writing, pinpointing the criteria that they hope to achieve in their drafts.

When students manage to get the chatbot to generate an essay that resembles the paper they are working on, it may be helpful to print it out so that they can examine it closely.

2. With the printout of the chatbot-generated paper at hand, students can use reflective writing to think through the question of what they can learn from the chatbot about the structure and content of the writing project they are developing, as well as the question of how to incorporate these ideas into their own writing.

In an open-ended reflective freewriting exercise, students can respond to some of the following questions:

★ What does the chatbot paper do well?

★ What good ideas did it have that you hadn't thought of already?

★ What good ideas did it have that you *had* already thought of?

★ What is different about the chatbot paper from the one you are envisioning?

- How can you go beyond what the chatbot has written in any of the following ways:
    - Ground your discussion in the question of what this topic means to you personally, to your loved ones, or to your community.
    - Write the paper in a way that foregrounds your own personal experiences with the topic.
    - Write the paper in a way that foregrounds your own process of learning about the topic and discovering new ways of thinking about it.
    - What could a chatbot never know about your topic? Foreground that aspect of your topic.
    - How can you apply your human perspective to tease out the complexities behind the canned analysis provided by the chatbot?
- If the chatbot essay perfectly matches the essay you were intending to write, how can you revise your approach to make it more personal and unique?

After students have had a chance to address these questions in writing, a full class discussion in which they summarize and compare their impressions can provide students with a range of ways of thinking about and answering these questions.

 Composition Connection

The mechanical, clunky way that chatbots adhere to the standards of conventional writing (in the case of academic writing, these conventions include features like introductory paragraphs

> with a thesis in the final sentence, body paragraphs with topic sentences and subpoints, formats for quoting and citing sources, and summative concluding paragraphs) makes those standards much more visible than they usually are, and, for this reason, chatbot-generated compositions provide useful sample texts for discussing what these conventions look like and how they function in a piece of writing.

3. Following this class discussion, students can return to the outlines for their writing project and revise them in ways that make them "AI-informed." This process may involve:

   ★ adding new relevant perspectives or information suggested by the chatbot

   ★ borrowing structural strategies from the chatbot essay, involving decisions such as how information is arranged into paragraphs or how paragraphs are ordered

   ★ incorporating new observations that are not directly borrowed from the chatbot essay itself, but from the student's reflections and discussion about the chatbot essay

   ★ tweaking the approach to the material to foreground more personalized or contextualized ways of writing the essay

   ★ rethinking the entire essay to personalize or humanize the student's approach to the material

   As they did after writing their reflection essays, students should have a chance to talk about the revisions they made to their outlines with a partner and/or as a whole class.

 **AI Aside**

The world has been justifiably astonished by the versatility, eloquence, and even quirky humor of AI-generated text. At the same time, it is also easy to recognize the impersonal, stereotyped quality of chatbot prose, which, of course, is simply a mash-up of sentences that have been written previously by millions of people. Even when chatbots are being poetical or humorous, their output is the discursive equivalent of the faceless mass personality that Heidegger called "the they," the anonymous voice of inauthenticity. Of course, chatbot technology will continue to grow more sophisticated, but it is, by definition, impossible for chatbot writing ever to express anything aside from its anonymous rehashing of what "they" say or have said. Someday, AI programs might break away from their reliance on the history of human literary input, but then they would be humanoid individuals who could benefit from sitting in a writing class alongside human students to develop their newly personalized voices. Chatbot writing in no way replaces human writers; conversely, it provides a vivid counterexample demonstrating what is valuable and necessary about human writers.

4. Students draft out an essay from their revised outline.

ADDITIONAL SUGGESTION:

A similar activity can enhance any aspect of the writing process. After students brainstorm an idea, feed the brainstorming prompt into a chatbot to see what the chatbot says that the humans didn't think of as well as what the humans said that the chatbot didn't think of. The results of human research are likely to differ in revealing ways from the results of chatbot research—and, of course, humans have access to forms of research (introspection, personal interviews, social observation, etc.) that chatbots do not have. In the revision process, it is interesting to contrast a chatbot's feedback on a student essay with the feedback that comes from classmates and instructors. All of these discussions are opportunities both to think through aspects of the writing process as well as to think metacognitively (that is, about thinking itself).

Revision

While the layout of this book suggests a linear progression through the stages of the writing process, the role of revision in composition serves to remind us that writers are always going back, rereading, rethinking, and rewriting. Revision is not just part of the writing process, it is its soul and guiding principle—the core of what it means to think about writing as a process: an unfolding, a going back to go forward, a timeless act of creation, a reflective loop where what is said is always relativized by a critical consciousness that is constantly assessing what is said, the splitting of the writer into subject and object, into doer and perceiver, speaker and critic, the soul of skeptical self-awareness. Revision is a chance not just to "correct mistakes," but to achieve a new perspective on your own ideas, to listen to the sound of your own words, and to find the places where your perceptions intersect with the perceptions of other people—instructors, classmates, and the world beyond.

The spirit of revision brings the entire writing process to life. There is a sense in which all of the stages of the writing process happen simultaneously and are nested inside one another; when a student develops an outline, for example, they are also brainstorming, researching, maybe drafting out some preliminary sentences, and, most importantly, revising as they go along so that new ideas are not simply added on but incorporated in ways that influence the shape of the emerging work. The revision process itself also draws on all these other skills, as writers brainstorm alternative ways to look at their topic, conduct research to bolster an argument, reconsider the way their composition is organized, and draft out alternative ways of expressing their ideas. The revision stage is an ideal time to reflect on the inter-embeddedness of all the stages of the writing process. While it is helpful for heuristic or pedagogical purposes to isolate and serialize these stages, in practice they are always happening in complex interaction with one another.

Even the term *revision* itself conceals a range of meanings. The proofreading style of revision is indeed an important skill for students to master, but the cognitive work involved in editing sentences for clarity and precision is completely different from that demanded by the more "profound" kind of revision, which may involve rethinking the basic conceptual premises. Although the term *revision* is frequently used to refer to both of these activities, they are actually complete opposites, one devoted to finalizing a piece of writing and the other to deconstructing it. Moreover, both of these modes of revision reflect back on each other as writers switch back and forth between the detailed textures of the individual parts and the macrostructure of the whole.

In short, revision processes are as varied and as complex as writers themselves, and UDL principles provide helpful guidance for embracing this variety and complexity. In a sense, no writer really understands what they have written until they see it reflected back to them through a different perspective. A UDL-informed revision process encourages student writers to solicit and respond to feedback from multiple audiences—peers, instructors, and outside readers—and to experiment with possibilities for expressing their ideas in other media. It provides them with opportunities to reflect on both the style of their writing voice and the deep architecture of their ideas, and it leaves the door open to future iterations and evolution of their ideas. The following activities provide a few simple strategies for providing students with opportunities to think about their writing in new ways, and to support them as they use these new perspectives to enrich their understanding of the world and of themselves.

Steered Peer Review

Guest activity by Cynthia J. Murphy

Research shows that peer review of writing, when steered intentionally, is an effective practice to improve student writing skills. Specifically, three distinct best practices yield the greatest results. Peer review is most effective when it is guided, made up of multiple peers, and reciprocal (meaning that students play the role of both reviewer and reviewed). Scaffolding students' writing via novice-to-novice interactions helps facilitate student understanding of course concepts. Steering peer review in a clear and manageable way that allows students to exchange feedback with multiple peers promotes the conditions necessary for student acquisition of improved writing, collaboration, and evaluation skills.

 UDL Overview

When students become part of the construction of one another's writing, the classroom environment becomes much more collaborative, generating new possibilities for engagement, expression, and critical thinking. Peer review opportunities, where students have exposure to multiple writing samples and various ways to approach a writing assignment, allow them to become more reflective and engaged in deep thinking around writing. Establishing specific guidelines for both reviewer and reviewed equalizes these student interactions.

GOAL:

Encourage students to make themselves understood by peer readers and writers; be receptive to making and suggesting audience-centered revisions; and take a collaborative, problem-solving approach to co-constructed writing.

YOU WILL NEED:

- ★ face-to-face class time or a videoconferencing app that features breakout rooms
- ★ guided instruction using the Praise, Critique, Instruct, Praise (PCIP) method of peer review featured in this chapter

TIME:

Twenty to thirty minutes (for any writing assignment, use this class activity as part of the revision stage of the writing process)

OUTCOMES:

Students will:

- ★ interact with peers to scaffold and contextualize learning about writing
- ★ take on the role of reader, provide suggestions, and benefit from peer feedback
- ★ practice decision-making, critical reflection on their writing, and collaborative partnership building
- ★ practice navigating peer review discourse, a convention of the field of writing and in any academic or workplace situation where peer evaluation is commonplace
- ★ deepen learning by taking an active role in the learning process and hone important interpersonal skills

Composition Connection

Instructors might not make course content as accessible as peers because of the very nature and underlying complexity of their knowledge. However, students function more at a similar level to one another and can share advice about writing strategies that instructors might take for granted. Collaboration, therefore, results in improved achievement along with a myriad of other benefits, such as scaffolding learning, providing a bridge between expert and novice content, promoting active and reflective learning, and providing the opportunity to improve collaboration skills that resemble professional writing situations and that are important for academic and career success. Finally, peer review is a self-regulatory activity whereby students play an active role in their own learning. This, in turn, increases their self-efficacy and raises their academic achievement.

DIRECTIONS:

For this activity, use the PCIP method of peer review, which has just four simple steps: (1) Praise, (2) Critique, (3) Instruct, and (4) Praise. Guided peer review such as the PCIP method provides students with active support.

Some important considerations as you facilitate this activity include:

★ The peer review is a formative assessment only, meaning students review one another's papers in progress; they do not grade the final draft.

★ Students should each bring in one page or less of their paper draft so the activity is manageable.

- ★ The errors writers make on a page of writing are often the ones they continue to make, so one page should be enough for readers to get a good sense of what they need to work on.

- ★ Encourage students to take notes and listen as they are playing the reviewee role. By listening to the feedback and not interrupting, students will get the most out of the review.

1. Praise. Form small groups of three to four students so students can read at least two other papers and receive at least two reviews. If meeting remotely, pair students with two to four peers using the breakout room feature or a comparable online platform to create small, private meeting spaces for students. Zoom, Canvas, Microsoft Teams, Google Chat, or similar tools can all work well. Instruct students to take five minutes to read one peer's work, taking turns reviewing one peer's paper at a time. When they have finished reading, some prompts for step 1 (Praise) include the following:

    - ★ What specifically do you like about the piece of writing?

    - ★ What writing strategy does your peer use that you would use in your own papers?

    - ★ What word, phrase, sentence, or paragraph stands out the most as well written?

    - ★ Identify a section of the writing where your peer followed the writing assignment instructions.

    - ★ Where does the writing flow best?

    - ★ Where do you see a full description, a good example, or complete paragraph support?

    - ★ What new information did you learn?

UDL Insight

This activity aligns particularly well with the UDL principle of fostering collaboration and community. Students are put into small groups to discuss their writing, and each member is given the specific roles of reviewer and reviewee and explicit instructions of what they are required to do, fostering successful peer interaction. Grouping peers together with clear objectives supports cooperative peer interactions.

2. Critique. Let students know that you will be available for questions, but you can reduce intimidation by busying yourself with work while students interact. If the class is working remotely, send messages to all breakout rooms letting students know how much time they have remaining and that you will remain in the main room for questions. When step 1 is complete, they now need to detect just one or two areas in need of attention.

    The critique should focus on:

    ★ a global issue (content, coherence, structure) over a local issue (grammar, punctuation, spelling)

    ★ a specific word, phrase, sentence, or small section

    ★ just one or two areas in need of attention per reviewer

    ★ areas in need of development that need an example or more explanation

    ★ questions that come up that need clarification

    ★ what they hope as a reader to understand or connect to

    ★ anything else they can think of

    Students should highlight or underline the confusing or problematic section(s) they detect. Specifically drawing attention to the area they believe needs work is more likely to result in feedback that students actually use. If meeting remotely, students can make marginal comments using an online notation feature, chat box, Microsoft Word or Google Doc feedback tools, or a text box.

3. **Instruct.** This step allows students to explain or give the reasoning behind their critique. In providing a rationale for their review, students are allowed to diagnose and verbalize the problem, figure out a solution, and again verbalize that solution to their peer.

To help students make specific diagnoses, you can provide:

★ an infographic of the main types of writing issues, their definitions, and examples

★ a sample student peer-reviewed paper with marginal notes

★ a short video tutorial of students engaged in peer review

Instructions should guide students to focus on no more than three global concerns (such as organization, coherence, and substantial content) over surface features (such as grammar and punctuation). Rubrics can help with this step.

 AI Aside

Chatbots can also be employed as peer editors. If you feed a draft of an essay into a chatbot and ask it to provide feedback on the strengths and weaknesses of the writing sample, it will generate a response. It may be instructive to ask students to compare the feedback they get from their classmates with feedback they get from the AI, in terms of both the content of the feedback as well as its tone. This kind of human/chatbot matchup typically demonstrates the mechanical, detail-oriented, and imitative style of chatbot thinking compared to the empathetic, gestalt, contextualized style of human thinking.

4. Praise. Finally, students should leave the peer review with a summary of their assessment with both suggestions for improvement and a final praise comment to reinforce the spirit of collaboration and end on a positive note. Any notes that accompany live dialogue should be easy to access and positive to help students comfortably receive an evaluation and focus on growth.

 UDL Insight

Playing the roles of reviewer and reviewee interchangeably offers students a means for self-regulation, deeper understanding of content, and increased transfer of knowledge. Providing feedback as the reviewer activates prior knowledge and allows students to see errors more clearly in their own writing, thus maximizing learning. Receiving timely and specific feedback as the reviewee also offers opportunity to deepen understanding, benefit from scaffolded learning, and take away clear directives on what to work on.

ADDITIONAL SUGGESTIONS:

★ The Steered Peer Review activity is particularly helpful if you set clear goals for the writing assignment, offering rubrics and clear written instructions to help drive the peer review. In addition, examples of successful student writing and writing in need of improvement will help students understand the assignment expectations.

★ It's a good idea to instruct students on the PCIP method beforehand, with an outside sample piece of writing they can practice with to help minimize risks and interpersonal distractions that could result from critiquing a peer's writing for the first time.

★ You can optimize outcomes by offering the PCIP method of peer review instruction in stages, devoting one class (or part of class) to teaching and practice on a writing sample, and devoting the next class (or part of class) to this Steered Peer Review activity on students' own drafts.

★ You can optimize student engagement with this activity by reminding them that evaluation skills such as the ones they will practice with the PCIS process are skills that are required not only in college classrooms, but also in the workplace.

"Wraparound" Feedback and Guided Revision

Guest activity by Nicole Brewer

How can writing teachers provide effective feedback to novice writers? This activity guides students through the revision stage of the writing process by offering alternative ways to help student writers not only better understand instructor feedback but also effectively address it.

Editor's note: This activity can be used for an assignment in which students are asked to write a full draft of an essay. This would work best for a first major writing assignment or any high-stakes writing project that involves students receiving written feedback from an instructor before completing a final version.

 **UDL Overview**

This activity uses multiple means of engagement by giving students comprehensive, detailed feedback on their writing and encouraging them to reflect on the feedback received and the

> writing process itself. The activity also uses multiple means of representation by providing students with feedback in both written and multimedia forms. It is designed to provide "mastery-oriented feedback" that highlights the importance of students' effort and improvement as part of the revision process.

GOAL:

Help students effectively use instructor feedback to revise a piece of writing.

YOU WILL NEED:

★ a slide presentation program, such as PowerPoint or Google Slides

★ video-recording or voice-recording capabilities

★ a computer lab for in-class work (optional)

TIME:

Three or four class sessions

OUTCOMES:

Students will:
- ★ draft a piece of writing
- ★ interpret instructor feedback
- ★ reflect on the drafting, revising, and editing experience
- ★ use instructor feedback to guide their revision process
- ★ revise a piece of writing

DIRECTIONS:

1. Ask students to write a draft of a major writing assignment for the course. Encourage them to write a completed draft that they have edited, revised, and proofread to the best of their ability.

> **AI Aside**
>
> A chatbot can also serve as a peer reviewer. Ask a chatbot to "evaluate the following essay," and then copy and paste the draft into the prompt box. The chatbot will provide some feedback that is very helpful, some that is vague and unconstructive, and some that may seem completely off the mark. Taking time to think through the validity of the chatbot's critique can be a great way both to get a new perspective on a draft and to learn more about what chatbots do well and what they don't do so well.

2. Once students complete a full draft of the essay, ask them to reflect on their writing and drafting experience by sharing two challenges and two successes they had while writing it. These challenges should relate to issues they have with the draft that they would like help addressing during the revision process. For example, a student could indicate that they had difficulty writing their introduction and need guidance on strengthening its opening sentences. The successes should convey aspects of the essay about which students feel proud or difficulties with the writing process that they have overcome. For example, a student could reveal that they were able to complete the assignment on time without feeling rushed by creating an essay writing plan.

UDL Insight

Asking students to reflect on their experience and to draft a piece of writing by indicating the challenges they faced during the writing process helps them develop self-assessment and reflection (9.3). This self-regulation Guideline is part of the UDL principle of engagement.

3. Provide students with traditional written feedback on their writing submissions. When giving feedback, be sure to address the challenges students mentioned in their drafting reflection and, if applicable, note the successes the students shared.

   Students may have trouble reading handwritten feedback, so consider providing them with electronic feedback through an LMS or even using tracked changes and comments in a word processing program like Microsoft Word.

4. Record a three-to-five-minute video for each student related to the comments on their papers. The video should be an overview or summary of your feedback on their papers instead of an in-depth explanation of each piece of feedback. Students tend to avoid watching lengthy videos; therefore, short videos are highly recommended. Be sure to briefly address challenges students mention in their drafting reflection. The videos can be recorded and then uploaded on YouTube. The link to the recorded video can be sent to students through email or an LMS.

5. Assign students to review the feedback they received on their draft as homework and write down or submit three questions they have about their draft and the feedback they received. This step can also

be completed as an in-class activity if students are able to meet in a computer lab during class time. You can ask students to review the feedback on a computer or their phones using headphones.

> **UDL Insight**
>
> Holding group student conferences or revision sessions encourages collaboration and community because students can guide and support one another through the revision process (8.3). This Guideline, which focuses on cooperation, collaboration, and community, is part of the UDL principle of engagement.

6. Conduct short (10–15 minutes) individual meetings with students to address their three questions about the feedback they received. These meetings can occur during class time or in your office. During these meetings, you can also dedicate time to helping students address specific comments on their papers. For example, if you commented "provide more examples," you can discuss specific examples with the student that would help strengthen the paper's argument. You may also find that groups of students are dealing with similar issues; therefore, you may decide to hold small-group conferences with students who are struggling with the same concepts. These small-group meetings, which can be held in lieu of or in addition to one-on-one meetings, may provide additional opportunities for student collaboration.

7. As part of the meeting process, assign students one comment or set of comments to address as homework or in-class work. The comments or set of comments to address can be determined collaboratively during a short meeting with each student or small student group; or, if the class as a whole is having trouble with one writing concept,

you can suggest that all students address one particular issue in their papers. For example, if most students are struggling with academic citation, you might require students to choose a single paragraph in their essay and direct students to address the citation issues for that paragraph as a homework assignment or in-class work activity.

8. Review students' revision work on the assigned section or paragraph of their essays. Provide simple feedback in the form that works best for you and the students—you can provide written, multimedia, or in-person feedback. Consider providing feedback in multiple ways to best benefit students. For example, if you're teaching an asynchronous online course, you might decide to provide both written feedback and video feedback to all students, whereas if you're teaching an in-person course, you might choose to provide written feedback and in-person feedback through short one-on-one meetings with students during class time.

 Composition Connection

This step allows students to apply what they have learned from your feedback and receive support during the application process. It also allows you to monitor students' understanding of the feedback they received as well as measure their ability to apply their knowledge by reviewing their revision work *before* they submit the assignment for a grade. The mini-revision portion of this activity can be especially important for novice writers who sometimes struggle to effectively utilize instructor feedback.

9. Once students receive their additional feedback on their mini-revisions, assign the final version of the essay that will be evaluated for a grade.

ADDITIONAL SUGGESTIONS:

★ You can enhance this activity by encouraging students to develop a clear writing process (i.e., brainstorming, drafting, revising, editing, and proofreading). This activity should be considered an in-depth look at the revision stage of the writing process. In the weeks before starting this activity, you may want to review the different stages of writing and encourage an open classroom discussion about students' own writing processes and address any questions or misconceptions they have about the writing process.

★ Provide beginning writers with a feedback dictionary or a handbook that defines common terms, phrases, and symbols that they may encounter when reviewing your feedback. Review this dictionary or handbook in class. You may want to create the handbook collaboratively with students as an in-class activity. Consider restricting this dictionary or handbook to a one-page/one sheet for students' ease of understanding and access.

★ For more advanced writers, you can omit or revise steps 7 and 8. For example, students in an undergraduate capstone course or in a master's-level course may not require the mini-revision assignment. In such a case, you may want to provide the mini-revision and additional feedback as an option for students who require or request additional assistance.

★ Novice writers often require additional support and motivation when revising their writing. If you have access to a computer lab during class time, consider completing some of the steps as part of classwork instead of homework. Steps 2, 5, 6, and 7 can all be completed as part of in-class work.

Publish and Flourish

The availability of publication opportunities on the internet allows people who happen to be students in a writing class to instantly transform themselves, as if by magic, into novelists, pundits, critics, commentators, social media personalities, content creators, and other types of expert rhetoricians. Students who publish their work are no longer "students" at all, but professional public figures operating on an equal footing with established thought leaders, and this activity is designed to coach them through the process of achieving this transformation.

 UDL Overview

In the absence of publication, writing can seem like pointless busywork, and in some sense this is an accurate assessment. While writing can serve many diverse psychological and intellectual purposes, one of its most important features is its ability to communicate ideas to an audience. Encouraging students to submit their work for publication optimizes the "relevance, value, and authenticity" of the composition process, while also affirming students' prerogative to assert their own expertise and claim their own voice.

GOAL:

Support students through the process of disseminating their scholarship.

YOU WILL NEED:

A website or LMS for hosting links to publication outlets.

TIME:

Two to three weeks

OUTCOMES:

Students will:
- ★ consider the genre of their own work and how it fits into the rhetorical landscape of published content

- ★ become familiar with the diversity and multimodality of the contemporary rhetorical environment
- ★ practice examining publications for information about submission procedures
- ★ identify a potential publication opportunity for their work
- ★ evaluate the style of their own work as it compares with the style of other work published by a specific publication outlet
- ★ revise their own work to adapt to the house style of a specific publication outlet
- ★ follow specific instructions for submitting their work for publication
- ★ reflect on the process of submitting their work for publication

 AI Aside

Student writers are unlikely to be familiar with the various publication outlets that exist for the kind of writing they're doing, but chatbots, with their digital fingers in the pie of online discourse, can provide helpful guidance when it comes to identifying publication opportunities. Ask a chatbot, "What is a good place to publish a research paper about addiction treatment?" or "Where can I submit experimental poetry for publication?" Once a student gets some leads from the chatbot, they can visit the websites of the suggested publications to see which outlet might be the best fit for their work.

DIRECTIONS:

1. As a class, survey the landscape of publication and dissemination opportunities for the kinds of writing that the students are doing. Since this landscape is always changing, this conversation allows you to bring yourself up to date regarding available venues for student writing at the same time that it introduces students to the diverse range of outlets that they might consider submitting their work to. The conversation should consider:

   ★ listservs posting calls for papers (CFPs) for journals

   ★ local news outlets, online newspapers, and community newsletters

   ★ on-campus digital and print publications (literary reviews, school newspaper, school blog page, etc.)

   ★ online publications specializing in the kinds of topics that students are writing about

   ★ conference announcements for presentations and posters

   ★ websites and blogs that accept submissions

   ★ social media sites

   ★ opportunities for digital self-publishing

   If the students are all writing about a similar topic, this conversation can focus on publications and websites that specialize in this topic. If the students' topics are more wide-ranging, the conversation can showcase the variety of dissemination possibilities available to writers.

   As the class visits the web pages for some of these different kinds of publication, show students how to find information on these websites about submitting writing. Publication outlets that accept work for submission typically have a link at the top or bottom of their home page labeled "Information for Authors" or "Submission Procedures." Encourage students to look for these links to determine whether a given outlet will consider their work for publication.

2. As an independent homework assignment, students can use the techniques discussed in class to identify an outlet that accepts submissions for the kind of writing they are doing. Students should post to an LMS discussion board the link to a web page specifying the submission procedures.

 Composition Connection

Surveying the house styles preferred by different editors and publications provides a dramatic lesson in the diversity of rhetorical forms and situations. Successful writers are not those who have mastered some particular formula or set of rules; rather, they are flexible and adaptive. They are responsive to contexts, and they bend their style to fit the expectations of different audiences. When students do all their writing for a single instructor who represents their only audience, it is easy to disregard this essential competency, but when they write for publication, the value of rhetorical versatility becomes readily apparent.

3. When the class reconvenes, lead a discussion about the dissemination opportunities identified by the students. Scrolling through the discussion board, visit the web pages that students have posted links to. This conversation is an opportunity for the class to survey the different kinds of submission criteria and procedures that different outlets recommend.

You should also use this opportunity to navigate from the "submission" page to examine the style of the kinds of content the outlet publishes. CFPs and conference presentations don't offer this possibility, but blogs, online publications, academic journals, and local journalistic outlets typically provide numerous examples of the house style preferred by the editors.

As the class visits these sites and looks through their content, students can analyze this house style, taking note of such features as:

★ average word count

★ level of formality

★ paragraph length

★ vocabulary

★ citation format

Preparing their work for publication may require revising what they have already written so that it conforms to both the stated and implicit style favored by the target outlet.

4. As homework or as a guided in-class writing project, students revise their work for submission to the target outlet. The purpose of this revision process is not primarily to correct technical issues or to enhance the draft's rhetorical effectiveness, but rather to shape the work so that it looks and sounds like the other content published by the outlet.

In some cases, this might mean rewriting their work as a pitch or an abstract, composing a cover letter and bio to accompany the submission, or doing any other kind of work instructed by the submission procedures. In other cases, it may mean reducing the word count, splitting up paragraphs, altering the tone of the piece, or making other changes to the draft itself.

5. In a show-and-tell-style series of presentations, invite students to discuss how they adapted their work for submission. These presentations will give students a chance to reflect on their own revisions, and it also gives the class as a whole a chance to consider the different rhetorical choices suggested by different contexts.

   Alongside these presentations, you can also serve as an editor, working with the student author to produce a final draft that is ready for publication.

6. Students submit their work for publication according to the procedures specified by individual publications.

 UDL Insight

Helping students publish their work "heightens the salience of goals and objectives" (8.1) of a writing class in ways that demonstrate the power of self-expression to reach audiences, communicate ideas, raise awareness, and effect change.

7. A week or so following step 6, convene with students to discuss whether anyone has heard back about their submissions. This is a great opportunity for students to get an inside look at the world of professional writing. Invite them to share any correspondence they received regarding their submission, as well as their thoughts and feelings about the process. If any students manage to get their work published, encourage the class to support the student writer by sharing links to their work on social media. You may also reach out to the school's marketing department to promote and showcase these writers' success.

ADDITIONAL SUGGESTIONS:

★ For an alternate spin on this assignment, the class can self-publish an anthology of their work, either as a digital site or as a physical book, in which case they can work together to establish their own editorial criteria.

★ If this activity is being done toward the end of a writing class in which the students have written several different kinds of assignments, they might be asked to choose the piece that they like the best as the one they submit for publication.

★ At the same time, while it makes sense to think of this publication activity as a kind of capstone project for the end of the class, it is actually ideal for students to submit work for publication early in the run of the class, since this allows more time for students to hear back from editors and publishers about their submissions (a process that can often take weeks or months).

Talk Show: Featured Writers Segment

Writers typically appreciate opportunities to talk about their writing, especially in supportive settings and in conversation with curious audiences. Indeed, in some cases, a piece of writing itself is largely a means to the end of sparking dialogue about a particular subject. As writers discuss their work with a variety of audiences, they inevitably develop a deeper understanding of the topic they are writing about as well as of their own thoughts and feelings about it. This deepened understanding may inspire writers to go back and revise or reformulate what they had written, or to embark on new writing projects inspired by the conversations they have had about what they have written.

UDL Overview

When students participate in structured conversation about their own writing, they have the opportunity to express their ideas in an alternative medium of expression—semi-spontaneous dialogue with an attentive audience—but the most impactful benefit of this talk show–style activity is the way that it addresses the UDL Guidelines regarding self-regulation. Responding to questions about their writing in a public forum where they are regarded as experts reinforces "beliefs and expectations that optimize motivation," particularly the belief that their words matter and the expectations of the community that they have earned this recognition of their expertise through the quality of their writing and thinking. At the same time, as the student writer articulates responses to questions about their writing, they practice important skills in "self-assessment and reflection."

GOAL:

Provide student writers with an opportunity to claim ownership of their writing, to be recognized as public authorities, and to engage in dialogue with their readers.

YOU WILL NEED:

★ a couch, if possible

★ a video camera with a good microphone and video editing software (optional)

TIME:

Four or five class sessions

OUTCOMES:

Students will:

- ★ articulate questions in response to a piece of writing
- ★ respond to questions about their own writing
- ★ engage in structured dialogue about their own writing and the writing of their classmates
- ★ act as public representatives for the point of view expressed in their writing
- ★ reflect on their own writing process

 Composition Connection

Opportunities to reflect on the revision process itself—whether in writing, in a video essay, or in conversation with their peers or instructor (or both)—can often be more educationally meaningful than the production of the revised draft itself. Rather than being ancillary to the writing process, such reflection opportunities sit at the heart of why we teach writing in the first place. After all, most student writing is not intended for publication; it is meant to teach students the metacognitive lessons about where ideas come from, how they can be put together, and what they can be used to do. Developing student-centered opportunities for students to reflect on what they've written and to respond to questions about their writing can help turn the draft-feedback-revision process from a one-way set of mechanical instructions into a more meaningful and collaborative educational experience.

DIRECTIONS:

1. Explain to students that the class will be staging a talk show in which they will all play the roles of host, guest, and audience member. The theme of the talk show will be "Conversations with Writers." In their role as host, students will compose and ask questions about a classmate's essay; in their role as guest, they will answer questions about their own essay; and in their role as audience member, they will ask follow-up questions of the featured writers.

    It may be helpful to begin with an open-ended conversation about talk shows that the students are familiar with and the techniques that successful talk show hosts use to make their interviewees open up and keep an interview moving along in an animated way. The class may discuss best practices for talk show guests and audience members as well. Consider the differences between a talk show, usually filmed before a live audience, and a podcast interview, which is typically conducted without an audience. The class may generate a list of stock questions that an interviewer might ask a writer about their work (What inspired you to write about this topic? What challenges did you encounter while writing this work? How would you describe your writing process? What do you want people to think after they've read your essay?).

2. Randomly assign students to pairs. Both students in each pair should read their classmate's most recent writing assignment and prepare a list of three or four interview questions. Some of these questions may be from the stock list, but at least some of them should refer specifically to the piece of writing under discussion, inquiring into certain observations or arguments articulated in the piece of writing, asking the writer to expand on certain points, or asking them to reflect on specific quotations from their work.

    It is important to note that this activity is not a revision workshop in the traditional sense of making recommendations for the writer to improve the piece of writing. As they prepare their questions, the talk show hosts should assume that they are reading a finished work, one worthy of discussion and acclaim. The goal of the activity is to celebrate, promote, and expound upon the writer's ideas, not to cavil and nitpick. As a result of these conversations, the writers may indeed decide to continue developing the pieces of writing under discussion, but conversations should be oriented around recognizing the students' achievements rather than pinpointing perceived flaws and shortcomings.

 AI Aside

Students can use a chatbot to help them articulate interview questions. Feeding the target essay into a chatbot and asking it to generate interview questions based on the essay can be a helpful starting point for thinking through some of the issues raised by the piece of writing, and it can also supply student writers with an interesting perspective on the kinds of questions raised by their work. It is important to scan through these questions, however, to make sure they have not already been answered in the original essay and that they are consistent with the writer's point of view.

3. After both partners get a chance to write a list of questions about their partner's work, they should share their lists with each other and talk about the interviews they will conduct. The interviews will probably be more successful if students have a chance to prepare answers to the interview questions before the interview itself. Students should also feel empowered to reject any interview questions that they would rather not answer and to work with their partner to formulate alternative questions.

4. Students conduct the interviews. If you can get a couch into the classroom, that simple piece of furniture goes a long way to setting a "talk show" mood. Otherwise, participants can sit at a table in the front of the classroom or in angled chairs. The format should be something like this:

   a. The host provides a brief introduction of the writer and briefly summarizes the work of writing under discussion.
   b. The host asks their questions, and the guest answers them.
   c. The audience gets a chance to ask a few questions of their own.
   d. The host makes some closing remarks and ends the interview.
   e. The host and guest switch roles and do it again.

You may devise some system for incentivizing all students to ask questions during the audience participation segment of each interview (asking a certain number of questions may be a requirement for earning complete credit for the activity).

If students consent to be recorded, it may be worthwhile to set up a camera and let it run throughout the interviews. If there are time and resources to do so, the student pairs can work together to edit the footage from their interviews. The final cut of the interviews can then be posted to the LMS or to social media.

 UDL Insight

Answering questions in front of an audience is a useful professional skill, but it can also be very daunting for some students. For this reason, this activity is structured to provide "graduated levels of support for practice and performance" (5.3) with the inclusion of several steps that help to prepare students for the "public speaking" phase. Writing out their essay in advance helps them

> collect their thoughts about their topic, discussing the interview process with the whole class (step 1) helps them visualize what they are being asked to do, and talking through the questions with their partner in advance (step 3) gives them a chance to prepare what they want to say. This scaffolded approach to their public appearance, along with a supportive and nonjudgmental classroom community, helps students build the confidence to be able to act as a public spokesperson for their point of view.

5. Following their interview, students write a brief reflection essay about how their participation in the process affected their thinking about the topic they wrote about and about the piece of writing they produced and discussed. Did answering the interviewer and audience's questions result in new perspectives or insights? Did they feel confident in their role as public experts? What aspects of the interview process did they like, and what aspects challenged them? How did listening to their classmates discuss their work influence their ideas about the writing process or about anything else?

Students are welcome to compose their reflection essay in writing, but, of course, they should also be invited to do so in whatever other medium they prefer (audio, video, infographic, cartoon strip, photo essay, etc.). The point of this reflection piece is simply to give the student a chance to process their experience with the talk show activity.

ADDITIONAL SUGGESTIONS:

★ The Talk Show: Featured Writers Segment activity makes a fun and engaging final exam activity. The assignment can be expanded to cover an entire portfolio of student writing (as opposed to a single assignment), giving students a chance to ask and answer questions about their experience across the class, writing in different genres, interacting with their classmates, and developing their skills as writers.

★ Consider using the class's LMS to make the essays that the students are discussing available to everyone in the class. This will allow students in the audience to make connections between what the writers say in their interviews and what they have written in their essays, and it also gives them a chance to dig deeper into any essays that sound particularly interesting to them.

★ If any students feel intimidated by the prospect of answering questions in front of a live audience, invite them to record their interviews separately and then show the recorded interviews in class or simply make them available through the LMS.

★ If the class chooses to record the interviews and post them online, using an audio transcription function to generate subtitles or transcripts of the interviews can help make these recordings more accessible to more students.

Acknowledgments

This book is the culmination of a long, winding narrative bristling with interesting characters, inspiring educators, and good friends. In one way or another, everything in this book traces back to interactions I've had with students and colleagues over the course of my career.

My first full-time job as an English teacher was at Rogers Park Middle School in Danbury, Connecticut, where I had the opportunity to work under the supervision of Dawn Hochsprung, one of the school's assistant principals. I faced a number of challenges in the classroom, as do many first-year teachers, but Dawn took time out of her busy schedule to mentor me (and also to defend me against some of the other teachers who were less patient with my learning curve). In a time before UDL existed, she taught me to think about the goal and work backward from there to determine what students would do to meet it. She encouraged me to try new things and to meet the students where they are. If it hadn't been for her support, it is very likely that I would have left education altogether. Decades after we worked together, Dawn, then working at Sandy Hook Elementary School, became one of the first victims of the unspeakable tragedy that unfolded there on December 14, 2012. She was one of the best people I've ever known, and I think about her all the time. It is likely that book would not exist if it hadn't been for her ability to see past my early struggles and help me overcome them.

I owe my first encounter with UDL to Danielle Wilken. In her time as Dean of Academic Affairs at Goodwin University, Dr. Wilken was so impressed with the transformative effect that UDL pedagogy had on her elementary-school-age son that she initiated a successful program of inculcating UDL practice into Goodwin's institutional culture. The result of her efforts is that Goodwin is currently recognized as a hub of higher ed UDL innovation. Almost all of the faculty, and many of the administrators and staff, are trained in UDL and sustain ongoing discussion about how to design educational environments that include all learners. This handbook is largely an extension of these discussions, especially the stimulating discussions I've enjoyed with my fellow English professors at Goodwin, Phillip J. Fox, Brian A. Dixon, Cynthia J. Murphy, Elizabeth Lane, and John Kania.

My colleagues and I were able to tell some of our stories about this transformation in our 2022 book, *UDL University*. I would like to thank everyone who collaborated with me on that book, especially my co-editors, Nicole Brewer and Dana Sheehan, and the contributors: Kelli Goodkowsky, Amy Beauchemin, Annjanette Bennar, Robin L. Young-Cournoyer, Ellen Swider, Zachary Vincent Smith, Cynthia J. Murphy, Phillip J. Fox, Keith A. Carter, Karrie Morin, Michelle Dent, Lisa Coolidge Manley, and Sandi Coyne-Gilbert. Working with these teachers to develop *UDL University* helped me think more broadly about the applicability of UDL approaches. I am also grateful to Dean Diana LaRocca for the instrumental role she has played in cultivating UDL-inspired perspectives at Goodwin University. Working on *UDL University* also introduced me to the team at CAST Publishing, who have obviously played a significant role in bringing this book into the light of day. I am particularly grateful to David Gordon and Billie Fitzpatrick for their support and guidance.

I would also like to thank my colleagues at the University of Bridgeport, Amy Nawrocki, Eric Lehman, and Elizabeth Haas, who continually inspire me with their professionalism, inventiveness, and commitment.

Most importantly, I am grateful to my wife, Ann, also a teacher, and to my children, Tony and Sharilyn, for surrounding me every day with love, creativity, and purpose. Oh, and Sigmund the cat, for consistently putting out the vibe.

The Universal Design for Learning Guidelines

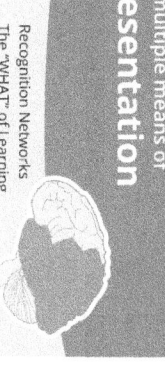

Provide multiple means of Engagement
Affective Networks
The "WHY" of Learning

Access

Provide options for Recruiting Interest (7)
- Optimize individual choice and autonomy (7.1)
- Optimize relevance, value, and authenticity (7.2)
- Minimize threats and distractions (7.3)

Build

Provide options for Sustaining Effort & Persistence (8)
- Heighten salience of goals and objectives (8.1)
- Vary demands and resources to optimize challenge (8.2)
- Foster collaboration and community (8.3)
- Increase mastery-oriented feedback (8.4)

Internalize

Provide options for Self Regulation (9)
- Promote expectations and beliefs that optimize motivation (9.1)
- Facilitate personal coping skills and strategies (9.2)
- Develop self-assessment and reflection (9.3)

Goal

Expert learners who are...

Purposeful & Motivated

Provide multiple means of Representation
Recognition Networks
The "WHAT" of Learning

Access

Provide options for Perception (1)
- Offer ways of customizing the display of information (1.1)
- Offer alternatives for auditory information (1.2)
- Offer alternatives for visual information (1.3)

Build

Provide options for Language & Symbols (2)
- Clarify vocabulary and symbols (2.1)
- Clarify syntax and structure (2.2)
- Support decoding of text, mathematical notation, and symbols (2.3)
- Promote understanding across languages (2.4)
- Illustrate through multiple media (2.5)

Internalize

Provide options for Comprehension (3)
- Activate or supply background knowledge (3.1)
- Highlight patterns, critical features, big ideas, and relationships (3.2)
- Guide information processing and visualization (3.3)
- Maximize transfer and generalization (3.4)

Resourceful & Knowledgeable

Provide multiple means of Action & Expression
Strategic Networks
The "HOW" of Learning

Access

Provide options for Physical Action (4)
- Vary the methods for response and navigation (4.1)
- Optimize access to tools and assistive technologies (4.2)

Build

Provide options for Expression & Communication (5)
- Use multiple media for communication (5.1)
- Use multiple tools for construction and composition (5.2)
- Build fluencies with graduated levels of support for practice and performance (5.3)

Internalize

Provide options for Executive Functions (6)
- Guide appropriate goal-setting (6.1)
- Support planning and strategy development (6.2)
- Facilitate managing information and resources (6.3)
- Enhance capacity for monitoring progress (6.4)

Strategic & Goal-Directed

CAST | Until learning has no limits

udlguidelines.cast.org | © CAST, Inc. 2018 | Suggested Citation: CAST (2018). Universal design for learning guidelines version 2.2 [graphic organizer]. Wakefield, MA: Author.

Index

A

academic journals, 28–29
accessibility
    of course materials, 28
    physical aids, 34–36
    of self-expression, 25–26
action/expression
    intellectual labor of, 32–34
    metacognition via, 39
    multimedia tools for, 159
    physical, 34–36
    in writing process, 13–14
adaptability, 3
AI (artificial intelligence)
    AI-proof writing activities, 3–6
    vs. articulation, 150
    brainstorming with, 85, 176
    collaboration with, 58, 170–177
    drafting with, 170–177
    human beings and, 128
    image generation by, 65
    interview questions from, 167
    lack of new ideas by, 80–81, 132
    opportunities with, 3–4
    outlines generated by, 139
    as peer reviewer, 190
    personal reflection on, 74
    research with, 109
    reverse engineering work by, 48
    vetting suggestions from, 116, 121
    writing style of, 176
analysis, 142–144
annotated bibliographies, 107
anxiety, 119
articulation, 150
assessments
    DIY options for, 59
    grading process, 22
    post-class, 69
    of prior knowledge, 27
    of reader comprehension, 54
    self-, 31, 63, 69
    Talk Show exam, 207
    of teacher effectiveness, 60
assignments
    low- to high-stakes, 161
    process vs. product, 21
audience
    feedback from, 30, 180
    for published work, 198
    revisions for, 182
    self as part of, 25
    talk about writing with, 201, 206, 208
audiovisual materials
    coursework via, 28
    for drafting, 37
    video scripting, 157–164
    vision board exercise, 61–70
    See also multimodality
awareness
    via graduated assignments, 161
    of interconnections, 159
    journaling for, 23
    as metacognition, 39–40
    vision board for, 61

B

bibliography, 107–112
blank page, 67, 126, 150
blogs, writing journal, 70–77
brainstorming
    AI help with, 85, 176
    explicit nurturing of, 94
    group, 87–88

brainstorming *(continued)*
    in a journal, 71
    Me-Time Log, 81–88
    Multidisciplinary Wonderball, 95–103
    with/for new ideas, 79–81
    productive, 81
    Random Facts Fantasia, 88–95
    UDL-informed, 13
    as uniquely human, 81
Brewer, Nicole, 188
building engagement, 21–22

C

calculators, 4
care and passions, 18, 82, 86, 129
CAST (Center for Applied Special Technologies), 3
chatbots
    asking questions of, 100
    collaboration with, 58
    drafting with, 170–177
    fear of/opportunities with, 3
    interview questions from, 167
    lack of new ideas by, 80–81, 132
    optimizing data from, 172
    outlines generated by, 139
    as peer reviewer, 186, 190
    personal reflection on, 74
    publication tips from, 196
    reverse engineering essays by, 48
    UDL-informed curriculum and, 7–8
    vetting suggestions from, 116, 121
    writing style of, 4, 176
cheating, 4–6
choice, 54
collaboration with chatbots, 58, 170–177
collaboration with peers, 181–188
Collaborative Paragraph Drafting, 151–157
communication
    in community, 22
    diverse forms of, 25
    intellectual labor of written, 34
    of learning, 18
    multimodal media, 2–3, 36–38
    via podcasts, 164
    for research, 113
    of technical information, 55
    tools for personal, 15
community
    of bloggers, 72
    collaborative drafting, 151
    DIY handbook to build, 52–61
    icebreaker profile to build, 45–52
    individual contribution to, 14
    journal blogs to build, 70–77
    for research, 22, 107, 111–112
    revising in, 192
    of topical interest, 119
    verbal presentations to, 111, 161
    vision board to build, 61–70
    writing classroom as, 44
Community Survey and Personal Interview, 113–119
complexity, 161, 180
composition
    central ideals of, 6
    digital vs. physical, 141
    email, 122
    objective, 134
    organizing a, 125–126
    by rote, 4
    in UDL context, 1–2
    See also writing
comprehension, 136
conceptual learning, 27
confidence, 38, 43, 94
connections, disciplinary, 95–103
content, students as, 43
content-oriented instruction, 26–27
contribution, individual, 14
conversation
    with an expert, 124
    feedback in, 32
    via podcast, 164–170
    Talk Show exercise, 201–208
core competencies, 34
course materials, 24
Covid-19 pandemic, 7
creativity
    of brainstorming, 81

via engagement, 17–19
as fundamental to writing, 12, 25
interdisciplinary, 96
as interesting, 16
rewarding, 22
of self-discovery, 4
as universally accessible, 26
critique, 185, 190
curiosity, 18
curriculum, 7–8

D

decision-making, 38–39
design, educational
inclusive, 44–45
for variability, 13, 19
dialogue, 80
digital publication, 51, 170, 194–201
disciplinary perspectives, 95–103
discussion
bibliographic, 107
in-class feedback, 32
feedback via group, 51–52
of me-time logs, 86
for research, 106
of vision boards, 67
of written work, 201–208
distractions, freedom from, 35
diversity
celebrating, 33
of organizational tools, 126
of research information, 106
welcoming student, 44–45
See also variability
DIY writing handbook, 52–61
drafting
AI-informed, 170–177
Collaborative Paragraph Drafting, 151–157
daunting nature of, 149
Instructional Video Scripting, 157–164
multimedia tools for, 37–38
outline/draft bridge, 140
Research Roundup Podcast, 164–170
UDL-informed, 14

E

ear, honing your, 26–27
editing
audio, 168
of emails, 123
feedback for, 31
by peers, 181–188
technical vs. topical, 180
of video presentations, 162
elocution, 163
Email an Expert, 119–124
email composition, 122
emotional engagement, 17–19, 85
empowerment
autonomous, 38
as expert learners, 119
by research, 106
via self-expression, 15, 43
via UDL, 1
via understanding ourselves, 6
of unique voice, 40
variable means for, 82
engagement
building on, 21–22, 134
how to access, 19–21
importance of, 17–19
internalizing, 22–23
via peer review, 181
social, 22
student and teacher, 16–17
sustained, 21–22, 87
via vision boards, 70
in writing process, 13–14
enjoyment of me-time activity, 84
environment, learning
physical considerations, 35–36
sense of community in, 44
essays
analyzing chatbot, 48
chatbot-generated, 173
writing icebreaker profile, 48, 49–50
ethical questions
of image-generating AI, 65
responsibility to subjects, 50
etiquette, social media, 124

evaluation, 135
executive function
    brainstorming as, 94
    importance of, 38–40, 64
    journaling for, 70
    teacher modeling of, 45
experience, variable, 12
experimentation, 12
expertise
    asserted via publication, 195
    expert learners, 53, 119–120
    mastery-oriented feedback, 189
    students as experts, 105, 107

F

facts, random, 88–95
fear, 1, 67, 126, 150
feedback
    dictionary for, 194
    drafting with, 38, 161
    on feedback, 30
    via group discussion, 51–52
    human vs. chatbot, 177, 186
    from instructors, 188–194
    multifaceted, 30–32, 180
    for novice or advanced writers, 194
    from podcast interviews, 169
    on research, 111–112
    Steered Peer Review, 181–188
    on vision boards, 69
    "wraparound," 188–194
focus, 35, 82

G

goals
    of cultivating unique voice, 40
    executive function for, 38
    feedback to realize, 32
    identifying personal, 54
    personal and topical, 21, 24–25
    process arriving at, 21–22
    self-discovery as, 22–23
    setting clear, 187
    vision board for, 66
Goodwin University, 6–7

grading, 16, 22
grammar
    DIY handbook for, 55–56
    tools to hone, 26–27
graphic layout, 54
group work
    brainstorming, 87–88, 94
    to create outlines, 136–138
    feedback via, 51–52
    on me-time logs, 86
    self-expression in, 36
    solitary work and, 155
    for vision boards, 67
guided revision, 188–194

H

habits
    identifying personal, 62
    journaling routine, 71, 75, 88
handbook exercise, 52–61
handwriting, 35
human beings
    and AI, 128, 186
    human thesis activity, 127–134
    idea generation by, 80–81, 132
    imagination of, 9
    passions/cares of, 18
    uniqueness of, 6

I

Icebreaker Profile, 45–52
ideas
    activities to stimulate, 8–9
    articulating, 150
    chatbot input for, 173–174
    confidence brainstorming, 94
    connecting life to, 87–88
    disciplinary perspectives on, 97
    how to access, 79
    journaling about, 23
    multimodal expression of, 36–38
    neurological integration of, 33–34
    new, as human, 132
    organization of, 125–126
    from random facts, 91–93

writing to generate, 72
written dissemination of, 18
identity
    and brainstorming, 80
    personal passions, 82
    as a writer, 39, 61–70
image-generating technology, 65
images, 65
imagination, 9, 150
inclusivity, 44–45
Index Card Shuffle, 140–147
information
    organization of, 141–144
    processing, 107, 136
    sources of, 109
inspiration
    identifying, 81
    from random facts, 88
institutional culture, 7
Instructional Video Scripting, 157–164
instructors
    assessing effectiveness of, 60
    creative engagement for, 16–17
    demonstrations by, 45, 48
    feedback from, 30, 31, 188–194
    idea-generating tools for, 9
    oversight/encouragement by, 50
    peers as, 186
    UDL mindset for, 16
intellectual labor, 32–34
interdisciplinary brainstorming, 95–103
interesting facts in Random Fact Fantasia, 89
interest(s)
    community of shared, 119
    Me-Time Log of, 81–88
    purpose via, 18
    research topics based on, 20
internalized engagement, 22–23
interviews, 46, 113–119, 165–168, 205
introspection, 80, 106, 126

J

jargon, 119
journals
    to develop voice, 72
    for executive function, 39
    Me-Time Log in, 84
    research, 23
    writing journal blog, 70–77

K

keyboards, 34–35
knowledge
    activating background, 136
    assessing previous, 27, 31
    gathering new, 109
    of peers, 183
    researching background, 105
    shared with the community, 49
    testing factual, 132
    writing as transforming, 33–34

L

layout
    for clarity/comprehension, 58
    for DIY handbook, 54
    of vision boards, 67
learning
    adapted to tech era, 3–4
    benefits of journals to, 70
    conceptual and performative, 27
    scaffolded, 1
    variability in, 12
letter writing, 122–123
listening
    to hone technique, 26–27
    for meaning/technique, 162–163
    text-to-speech tools, 35

M

math
    calculators for, analogy to chatbots, 4
    statistical data, role in composition, 118
meaning
    via engagement, 17–19
    finding topical, 133
    listening for, 162–163
    via personal passions/cares, 18
    for teachers and students, 16–17
    uniquely human, 128, 129

memory, 35
message, 2
metacognition
    via collaboration, 151
    via DIY handbook, 54
    and executive function, 38–39
    idea journal for, 23
    shared culture of, 70
    via writing, 15, 203
Me-Time Log, 81–88
mindset, UDL, 15–16
Multidisciplinary Wonderball, 95–103
multimodality
    activities encouraging, 5
    in community-building, 45
    for course materials, 24, 28
    in DIY handbook, 59
    vs. drafting, 149–151
    for feedback, 191
    for index cards, 147
    for journaling, 23, 74, 85
    in jumping-off points, 67
    in personal expression, 47
    podcasts and, 164, 168
    for research, 29, 106–107, 115
    for self-expression, 36–38
    Show-and-Tell Multimedia Bibliography, 107–112
    in UDL, 2–3, 12
    video scripting, 157–164
    in writing process, 21–22
Murphy, Cynthia, 180
My Human Thesis, 127–134

N

"natural" talent, 2
nonlinear learning, 24–25

O

objective compositions, 134
one-on-one conferences, 32, 192
online learning
    asynchronous/synchronous, 52, 102
    reliability of "facts," 95
    UDL-informed, 7
open-mindedness, 45
opportunity of AI, 3–4
organization
    diverse toolkit for, 125–126
    via index cards, 141–147
    of paragraphs, 153
    rhetorical, 2
original ideas, source of, 79–81
outlines
    by chatbots, 139
    for collaborative drafts, 152
    diverse toolkit for, 126
    Index Card Shuffle, 140–147
    My Human Thesis, 127–134
    as organized structure, 125
    outline/draft bridge, 140
    outsourcing your, 134–140
    from random facts, 93
    without research, 136

P

paragraphs
    collaborative drafting of, 151–157
    scripting, 162
    structuring, 153
parameters, narrow, 25
paraphrasing, 30
participation, 32
passions, personal, 18, 82, 86, 129
patterns, brainstorming, 101
PCIP (Praise, Critique, Instruct, Praise) method, 182, 183, 187, 188
peers
    community of, 44
    feedback from, 30
    learning about your, 49
    Steered Peer Review, 181–188
performative learning, 27
Personal Interview, 113–119
personalization
    of assignments, 6
    best work via, 19
perspective, personal
    artifacts to show, 47
    in collaboration with chatbots, 173–174

as the "content," 43
discovering/articulating, 15
diversifying, 89
as fundamental to writing, 25
impersonal and, 156
log to identify, 81
thesis via, 127–134
topics expressing, 20
uniqueness of, 14
perspectives, multiple, 144, 151
physical action, 34–36, 64
plagiarism, 1, 3, 150
podcasts, 164–170
PowerPoint, 59, 110, 147, 159, 160
praise, 184, 187
process, writing
    accessibility via, 2
    activities for, 8
    articulation of, 194
    for chatbot-era learning, 5
    DIY handbook on, 55
    drafting as part of, 149
    feedback in, 30
    increasing complexity in, 161
    multimedia tools for, 37–38
    nonlinear, 21, 24–25, 179–180
    research, 105
    as scaffolding, 1
    society to solitude in, 155
    UDL Guidelines in, 12–14
process assignments, 21
product assignments, 21
profile
    to break the ice, 45–52
    of an expert, 121–122
public speaking, 206
publication, 194–201
punctuation, 55–56
purpose, 18

Q

quantitative literacy, 118
questionnaires, 113–119
questions, interview, 167, 205

R

Random Facts Fantasia, 88–95
readings
    aloud, to hone technique, 26–27
    critical reading, 28
    decoding via, 29–30
    peer reviews, 181
    responding to, 27–30
recording scripts, 162–163
reflection
    for brainstorming, 81
    on drafting, 191
    to humanize research, 130–131
    via journaling, 70–71, 85
    metacognition and, 38–39
    multidisciplinary, 101
    via peer review, 181
    via talk about writing, 202, 203
    tools for personal, 77
    via vision boards, 69
relationships, brainstorming, 101
representation
    artifacts for personal, 47
    content-oriented instruction, 26–27
    of course materials, 24
    of research, 107, 111
    response to texts, 27–30
    variable modes for, 24–26
    in writing process, 13–14
research
    AI for, 109
    community for, 22
    Community Survey and Personal Interview, 113–119
    as a conversation, 164
    Email an Expert, 119–124
    finding meaning in, 133
    human vs. chatbot, 176–177
    humanizing, 130–131
    via index cards, 140–141
    interactive, 105
    journal for, 23
    new perspectives on, 96
    open-ended topics for, 19–20
    options in materials for, 28–29

research *(continued)*
  personalized topics of, 83
  random facts for, 91–92
  Research Roundup Podcast, 164–170
  response to sources, 27–30, 112
  Show-and-Tell Multimedia Bibliography, 107–112
  UDL-informed, 13
Research Roundup Podcast, 164–170
respect, 45
responsibility, 50
revising
  collaborative, 157
  defined, 180
  feedback for, 31
  human vs. chatbot feedback, 177
  as key to writing, 179–180
  post-feedback, 193
  for publication, 194–201
  Steered Peer Review, 181–188
  Talk Show exercise, 201–208
  UDL-informed, 14
  of vision boards, 69
  "Wraparound" Feedback and Guided Revision, 188–194
rhetorical structures, 144
rote composition, 4
routines, 71, 75, 88

S

scaffolding
  decoding texts as, 29–30
  outlines as, 126
  via peer review, 181, 182
scheduling writing, 36
scholarly texts, 28–29
scrambling information, 142
scripting videos, 157–164
self-assessments, 31, 172, 191
self-discovery, 1, 5, 15, 22–23
self-expression
  via composition, 2–3
  as the "content," 43
  via creative engagement, 17–19
  empowerment via, 15
  via journaling, 85
  joy of, 9
  multimodal, 36–38
  via publication, 200
  of style and voice, 72
  as universally accessible, 25–26
  via words, 149–151
  of writer personas, 64–65
  via writing, 1, 5, 32–33, 40
  writing about artifacts of, 47–50
self-publication, 201
self-regulation, 63, 70, 183, 187
Sheehan, Dana, 164
Show-and-Tell Multimedia Bibliography, 107–112
skill development
  of brainstorming, 94
  of composition, 24
  via journaling, 76
  writing as key, 34
slideshows, 37, 160
social environment
  drafting within, 38
  feedback within, 30
  multiple perspectives in, 144
  overwhelm by/in, 119
  research within, 113
  writing in, 22, 36, 146
  See also community
social media, 124
solitude, 22, 36, 146, 155, 170
sources, research, 107, 109, 110, 115
space, writing, 64
speech-to-text, 35, 162, 169
spontaneous response, 96, 101
statistical data, 118
Steered Peer Review, 181–188
storytelling, 146
structuring
  by chatbots, 174–175
  paragraphs, 153
  rhetorical, 144
students
  as the "content," 43
  emotional engagement for, 17–19

    as expert learners, 119
    peer feedback from, 30–31
        as research experts, 105, 107
    in writing community, 44
style, personal, 72
style, publisher, 198–199
subdisciplinary perspectives, 102–103
subjective writing, 134
submission for publication, 194–201
support, 44, 155
surveys, 113–119
sustaining engagement, 21–22, 87
synthesis, 142–145

T

Talk Show exercise, 201–208
"talking back" to sources, 112, 120
technical skills
    DIY writing handbook for, 52–61
    instructor response to, 31
    reading to hone, 26
technology
    adapted to education, 3
    to assist physical action, 34
    chatbots as assistive, 171
text-based composition
    daunting nature of, 149–151
    intellectual value of, 34
    UDL principles for, 2
texts
    decoding, 29–30
    email, 122
    research via, 110, 115
    responding to, 27–30
text-to-speech, 35
thesis
    collaborative outlines on, 136–137
    human, 127–134
thought
    as the "content," 43
    daily record of, 85
    emotional engagement as, 18
    expertise via novel, 120
    human, 186
    materials to provoke, 28
    stimulating metacognitive, 39
    thought experiments, 94–95
tone, establishing, 2
topics
    expertise on, 119
    finding meaning in, 133
    new perspectives on, 96
    open-ended, 19–20
    outlines on, 125
    publication by, 197
    student-determined, 83
    variability in approach to, 20
tutorials, DIY, 52–61

U

UDL (Universal Design for Learning)
    and adaptation to technology, 3–4
    assessments in, 60
    central ideals of, 6
    as creative and interesting, 16–17
    early adoption of, 7
    empowerment via, 1, 15
    journaling and, 70
    variability built into, 2, 19, 33
    in writing process, 12–14
UDL + 1 approach, 8
UDW (Universal Design for Writing), 12–14
uniqueness
    and new ideas, 79–81
    thesis on personal, 127
    of writer identities, 39–40
    in writing process, 12, 33
University of Bridgeport, 7, 8
usage, 26–27, 52–61

V

values, 81, 86, 129
variability
    among writers, 33
    celebrating, 89
    in collaborative drafting, 151
    in course materials, 28
    of engagement tools, 82
    for executive function, 39
    as fundamental to writing, 25

variability *(continued)*
- leveraged for new ideas, 80
- in lived experience, 6, 7
- in topics, 20
- as UDL foundation, 12–13, 19
- welcoming student, 44–45

vetting chatbots, 116
video lectures, 157
video scripting, 157–164
vision boards, 61–70
vocabulary, 26–27, 28
voice
- as accessible to all, 25–26
- asserted via publication, 195
- connecting spoken and written, 164
- development via journals, 72
- elocution and timing, 163
- empowering, 1, 33
- opportunities to encourage, 9
- reading your writing, 26
- safe space to enable, 45
- UDL tools for finding, 15
- welcoming diverse, 44–45

W

word prediction tool, 35
writers
- in community, 44
- ethical responsibility of, 50
- "featured writer" exercise, 201–208
- identity as, 39
- self-reflection exercise, 61–63

Writer's Vision Board, 61–70
writing
- about new ideas, 132
- AI-proof, 3–6
- as articulation, 150
- by chatbots, 176
- collaborative, 151–157
- as creative/variable, 12
- demystifying, 2
- dissemination of ideas via, 18
- engagement with, 17–19
- ethics of, 50
- fear of, 1
- journals, 23, 39, 70–77
- as multifaceted, 25
- organized structure of, 125
- physical action of, 34–36
- process approach to, 2
- publication of, 195
- in response to texts, 27–28
- revising as key to, 179–180
- as self-expression, 32–33
- as social, 22
- in UDL context, 2–3
- as universally accessible, 26
- vision board for, 61–70
- *See also* composition

writing instruction
- content-oriented, 26–27
- experimentation in, 12
- goal of, 9
- importance of, 34
- journals to enhance, 76
- and learning of "self," 32–33
- "legacy" practices in, 16
- personalizing, 19
- in post-chatbot landscape, 5–6
- representation of goals for, 24
- self-discovery via, 4–5, 15, 43
- social context of, 22
- on technical skills, 26
- UDL-informed, 16

Writing Journal Blog, 70–77
"writing what you know," 18–19

About the Author

Randy Laist, PhD, is a professor of English and chair of the English department at the University of Bridgeport. Laist received his doctorate in American literature from the University of Connecticut. He has taught in middle schools, high schools, and colleges, and his writing has appeared in the *New York Times*, *Salon*, and *The Chronicle of Higher Education*. He is also the co-editor of *UDL University: Designing for Variability across the Postsecondary Curriculum*.About the Author

About the Contributors

Nicole Brewer is the director of the Academic Coaching Center and an assistant professor of humanities at Anna Maria College in Paxton, Massachusetts. Her research focuses on reforming developmental education and academic support methods in higher education, and she has a specific interest in improving the college experience for historically underrepresented students. Her work as a scholar-practitioner can be found in the book *Faculty Development: Achieving Change Through Action Research*. She is also a contributor and a co-editor of *UDL University: Designing for Variability Across the Postsecondary Curriculum* (CAST, 2022), a collaborative volume of narratives about implementing UDL in a university setting.

In addition to her work in higher education, Nicole is dedicated to social justice initiatives. She collaborated with her father to write *Withstanding the Lie,* a book that offers strategies to help people cope with the mental and emotional harm caused by bigotry.

Cynthia J. Murphy is an associate professor of English and the director of English and philosophy at Goodwin University, where she has taught for two decades. She received a master of arts in English from Trinity College, and she is a PhD candidate in the College of Education at the University of Massachusetts, Lowell. Cynthia has received numerous awards of distinction in teaching excellence, service, and scholarship, including the National Institute for Staff and Organizational Development (NISOD) Excellence in Teaching Award. Her published scholarship includes a chapter in *UDL University: Designing for Variability Across the Postsecondary Curriculum* and the journal article "Disparities in the Likelihood of Earning a College Degree Among Students with Noncommittal, Low, and High

Educational Self-Expectations," published in the *Journal of Education for Students Placed at Risk* (JESPAR).

Cynthia has also won awards for fiction and poetry, and her creative work has appeared in numerous literary journals, including *Adanna Literary Journal* and *Icarus International*. She primarily teaches first-year composition, literature, and creative writing courses, and she lives on Lake Quinsigamond with her family in Shrewsbury, Massachusetts.

Dana Sheehan, MFA, has been working in higher education since 2008. As a tenure-track assistant professor of writing and director of the Anna Maria College Writing Center, she enthusiastically teaches English, writing, and communication courses. She has been working in writing centers since 2013 and opened new writing centers at two different institutions. Dana's Universal Design for Learning pedagogy helps her writing centers flourish by allowing all students, staff, and faculty to bring their own strengths to the centers in multiple ways.

Dana is also a co-editor of *UDL University: Designing Variability Across the Postsecondary Curriculum* and is working on her next book about the importance of creating community-driven writing centers.

More from CAST Professional Publishing

ISBN 978-1-930583-85-6 (Print)
ISBN 978-1-930583-86-3 (ePub)
210 PAGES | © 2022

UDL University: Designing for Variability Across the Postsecondary Curriculum

Edited by Randy Laist, Dana Sheehan, and Nicole Brewer, foreword by Allison Posey

"We know that our higher education institutions are not accessible or equitable for every student. UDL can help remedy that by enabling intentional design that supports physical, cognitive, and emotional access to learning."

—ALLISON POSEY, co-author of *Unlearning: Changing Your Beliefs and Classroom with UDL*

ISBN 978-1-943085-04-0 (Print)
ISBN 978-1-943085-05-7 (ePub)
208 PAGES | © 2023

Delivering Inclusive and Impactful Instruction: Universal Design for Learning in Higher Education

By Kevin L. Merry

"Kevin Merry helps postsecondary educators understand why and how they can design curriculum and instruction that is both inclusive and effective."

—KAVITA RAO, PhD, University of Hawaii at Manoa

ISBN 978-1-930583-96-2 (Print)
ISBN 978-1-930583-97-9 (ePub)
198 PAGES | © 2023

Upskill, Reskill, Thrive: Optimizing Learning and Development in the Workplace

By James McKenna

"Using Universal Design for Learning to understand and leverage variability across learners—in language, learning differences, disabilities, backgrounds and experience—McKenna outlines the considerable learning science underpinning the framework, and culminates with a detailed guide for applying UDL Guidelines. This is a great entry point to UDL for anybody involved in corporate learning and training."

—DENIS SAULNIER, Director of Digital Learning, Ariel Group

For more information, visit **www.castpublishing.org** or wherever books are sold. For bulk orders, email **publishing@cast.org**.

More from CAST Professional Publishing

UDL Now! A Teacher's Guide to Applying Universal Design for Learning, Third Edition

By Katie Novak, with a foreword by George Couros

"Katie Novak's well-articulated know-how, about how to put UDL into practice, has helped many thousands of educators. . . . She can describe what she does without evaporating the awe, the joy, or the sublimity of what great teaching is really like."

—DAVID H. ROSE, co-founder of CAST

ISBN 978-1-930583-82-5 (Print)
ISBN 978-1-930583-83-2 (ePub)
ISBN 978-1-943085-24-8 (Audiobook)
196 PAGES | © 2022

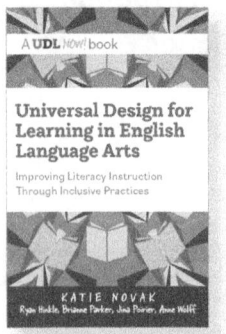

Universal Design for Learning in English Language Arts

By Katie Novak, Ryan Hinkle, Brianne Parker, Jina Poirier, and Anne Wolff

Katie Novak has teamed up with four literacy experts to offer educators a practical guide to integrating Universal Design for Learning in the English language arts classroom. The book demonstrates how to build rich, collaborative, and engaging literacy environments for students with varied backgrounds and needs.

ISBN 978-1-943085-08-8 (Print)
ISBN 978-1-943085-09-5 (ePub)
184 PAGES | © 2023

Transform Your Teaching with Universal Design for Learning: Six Steps to Jumpstart Your Practice

Jennifer L. Pusateri

"Putting UDL into practice can be daunting for teachers who are just starting out. Jennifer L. Pusateri puts them at ease as she suggests step-by-step strategies to transform our teaching with this powerful framework."

—ANDRATESHA FRITZGERALD, founder of Building Blocks of Brilliance LLC

ISBN 978-1-930583-95-5 (Print)
ISBN 978-1-930583-94-8 (ePub)
224 PAGES | © 2022

For more information, visit **www.castpublishing.org** or wherever books are sold. For bulk orders, email **publishing@cast.org**.

MORE FROM CAST

CAST is a nonprofit education research and development organization that created the Universal Design for Learning framework and UDL Guidelines. Our mission is to transform education design and practice until learning has no limits.

CAST supports learners and educators at every level through a variety of offerings:

- Innovative professional development
- Accessibility and inclusive technology resources
- Research, design, and development of inclusive and effective solutions
- Credentials for Universal Design for Learning
- And much more

Visit *www.cast.org* to learn more.

www.ingramcontent.com/pod-product-compliance
Lightning Source LLC
Chambersburg PA
CBHW081544080526
44527CB00010B/2